I highly commend this work l
Matthew Allen. Over forty years ag(
Ernie's associate pastor and then pastc
Church in Pompano Beach, Florida. T
work for the future Founder's Ministr. published his views in the church newsletter on the regulative principle, Christian liberty, and the biblical teaching on accommodation for the sake of preaching the gospel. I was privileged to learn much from him then.

This book summarizes the teaching of Scripture and church history, . . . especially documented Baptist history, . . . on the regulative principle of worship (Reformed) vs. the normative principle of worship (Lutheran and Anglican). The regulative principle champions commanded worship versus the normative principle of permitting what is not specifically prohibited. Indeed, Reisinger and Allen show how the very foundations of the Baptist movement rested on the regulative principle against infant baptism and uncommanded worship practices. They document this from Scripture and original sources.

This generation of Baptists and other evangelicals have often left the regulative principle and its commanded worship to introduce uncommanded practices that detract from and/or limit the preaching of the Word in worship. The modern appeal to human desires over biblically commanded worship has made worship more about the felt experience of the worshiper than worshiping God by faith as he has instituted it in the new covenant church (see 2 Tim. 4:1–4). This book draws the reader back to the biblical (and Reformed) doctrine of worship and offers correction to today's confusing scene in the church. One of the elements of regulated worship is the doctrine of Christian liberty, which is often ignored or misunderstood in the wars on worship, thus dividing sincere Christians. One of the best presentations of the right doctrine of Christian liberty is presented in this book. The authors apply it specifically to the regulative principle of worship to teach biblical worship and to correct its errors on all sides, both too restrictive and unrestrictive views. Their explanation of the difference between accommodation and compromise in worship practices is a valuable discussion, especially toward the great errors involved in the modern addition of the "altar call" system.

I do have one caveat for the reader: Ernie's commendation of John Frame for the regulative principle view was written before Frame introduced his errors concerning the elements of worship and the circumstances of worship in his work, *Worship in Spirit and Truth*. He changed the regulative principle to introduce plays, movies, interviews, dance, etc., as simply circumstances of the biblical command to preach the Word in worship, thus corrupting the practice of the regulative principle of worship and reducing the centrality of preaching in worship. Ernie can be forgiven for his commendation of Frame since these errors only became evident at a later time.

Overall, I commend the reading of this book to students, pastors, and the people in the pew to restore biblical worship to that which is commanded by God instead of invented by man's desires. After all, the best worship of God must be formed by his own commands concerning his worship.

– Fred Malone | Pastor Emeritus at First Baptist Church, Clinton, LA

WORSHIP

The Regulative Principle and the Biblical Practice of Accommodation

WORSHIP

The Regulative Principle and the Biblical Practice of Accommodation

Ernest C. Reisinger and D. Matthew Allen

FOUNDERS
MINISTRIES
CAPE CORAL, FLORIDA

Worship: The Regulative Principle and the Biblical Practice of Accommodation

Published by Founders Press

P.O. Box 150931 • Cape Coral, FL • 33915

Phone: (888) 525-1689

Electronic Mail: officeadmin@founders.org

Website: www.founders.org

Printed in the United States of America

ISBN: 978-0-9705248-6-7

Cover Design by Perry Brown

Interior Design by InkSmith Editorial Services

Contents

Foreword

The material in this book comes from the accumulated wisdom of years of practical ministry in the church. Under the best of circumstances, church life is a challenge. In days of widespread spiritual lethargy and downgrade, local church life and practice can seem almost beyond recovery. Yet, the New Testament makes it clear that even bad churches filled with wickedness are worth reforming (see Revelation 2 and 3).

The work of reformation is not easy, and it cannot be neatly scripted. Too many diverse situations arise to be covered in any comprehensive rule book. But some vital principles can shed light on the path for those who are highly committed to seeing a local church redirected in a God-honoring way. Identifying these principles is a large part of the initial work of reformation. Applying them is its ongoing work.

This book is helpful on both counts. By examining the principles of accommodation and regulated worship, the authors bring to light a number of issues that are fraught with difficulties when a local church gets serious about conforming to biblical practices. By heeding the counsel in the following pages, pastors and church leaders will see more clearly which battles are worth fighting and which are worth avoiding.

The sixteenth-century Reformers were convinced that the church must be "reformed and always reforming according to the Word of God." That conviction needs desperately to be recovered by a new generation of men and women who are committed to seeing local churches become all that God intends them to be. May this book be a catalyst to that cause.

–Tom Ascol

INTRODUCTORY COMMENTS ON *WORSHIP*

Worship according to the will and revelation of God is the most important vocation of God's image-bearers. The Ten Commandments include as the fourth commandment a particular day in which we are to do even as God did upon the completion of the execution of the first in the order of his decrees. When he finished creation, he stopped, observed, and admired it as "very good." The seventh day, then, was set aside as rest from labor to be spent in a state of blessedness and holiness (Gen. 2:2, 3).

Even so, the completion of the even greater work, decreed before the foundation of the world, the work of redemption by the Son of God, through whom all things were created, is now set aside as a day of blessedness and holiness. Though the spirit of edification should permeate the entire day, a time of corporate worship has been set aside as a prominent element of the Lord's Day, the Christian Sabbath, the day that rest was established for believers in the completed work of Christ (John 20:1, 19, 26; 1 Cor. 16:1, 2; Heb. 4:4-10; 10:24, 25; Rev. 1:10). The manner of worship and the various elements that should be included are presented with clarity and by example in the New Testament. Should we feel free to add anything to the worship of God beyond what God has prescribed through apostolic example and regulation? Some say, "Yes, we may add helps to worship beyond what is specifically prescribed as long as we do not include what is clearly proscribed or do something antithetical to love of God and love of neighbor." Such practice is called the normative principle. Others look at such supposedly benign additions as "will worship" or "self-imposed religion" or "self-made religion" (Col. 2:23). They observe that God has given specific practices to be included in Christian corporate worship either by example or command, thus allowing nothing beyond what he himself has required. This conviction gives expression to the regulative principle of worship.

This book presents a defense of the regulative principle. It narrates an overview of the nature of Christian worship and then defines the regulative principle as the guideline that most aptly captures the spirit of New Testament worship. The authors defend its solidly and thoroughly biblical character and give a history of its defense in the context of Reformed biblical exegesis and historic confessions. They pay special attention to its operation among Baptist commentators and theologians. The result of this careful work is a clear biblical and theologically sound presentation of the regulative principle of Christian worship.

Then the principle is applied to a specific evangelistic technique known as the invitation system. Their conclusion is that the system, as it is commonly presented as an ordained means of manifesting saving faith, violates gospel definitions of faith. As practiced in this way, it violates the regulative principle and, therefore, should be eliminated or altered radically. Immediate change, therefore, in obedience to Scripture must be executed on this practice along with other situations inconsistent with the regulative principle. The authors explore ways to defang the poisonous element while implementing gradual and sensitive amendments of existing patterns.

This reality prompted the authors to include a theological discussion of the principle of accommodation. Their discussion proceeds with great Christian sympathy and with wise recommendations as to how to remove the most glaringly unbiblical elements while still maintaining the expectation that the gospel always calls for the response of the sinner. It is filled with wise, biblically faithful, culturally sensitive advice on how to implement biblical accommodation.

This book is both a desideratum and a necessity for those who seek to plan biblically faithful worship for Christian congregations.

– Tom J. Nettles

Preface

How Shall We Worship?

This is a book about worship. Our purpose is to scrutinize the biblical foundation of how we worship. This is not an easy inquiry. Doing the subject justice involves more than merely pulling a few proof texts out of one's memory bank and contentedly resting one's case. We hope to go deeper than that. We hope to examine the theological basis for what we do when we worship. How should we worship? How should we conduct church? How can we go about determining whether our worship practices are biblical?

More specifically, this is a book about the forms of worship. Are there any proper forms of worship, and if so, what are they? When it gets down to specifics—yes, there's the rub. Specifics of how we should worship have engendered what some term "worship wars." Good men and women have vehemently disagreed over a number of specific worship practices. No one can even agree on the proper range of the debate. In some circles, the questions are whether we should sing uninspired hymns in worship services or whether we should have musical instruments to accompany the singing.

In other circles, the questions revolve around whether we should sing praise choruses or use drama alongside or in place of preaching. In still other circles, the questions are whether we are free to engage in "holy laughter" or being "slain in the spirit" or other manifestations of ecstatic experience. And in typical Baptist circles, of course, there is the question of the altar call.

With these questions comes a growing unease among many that contemporary evangelical Christianity is loosed from its theological moorings and drifting aimlessly in an ocean of relativism and uncertainty. This expresses itself in the area of worship in the incessant desire to always be "relevant" and "contemporary." Whether or not one agrees with the changes, John MacArthur is surely not off base in concluding that "the corporate worship of the Lord's Day is undergoing a revolution that has few parallels in all of church history."[1]

Finally, this is a book about Baptist worship. Historically, Baptists have enjoyed a rich history of reformed, and reforming, worship. In fact, most of our distinctives that separate us from other evangelical denominations arise in the area of worship. Although we are not sanguine about much of what passes as "contemporary worship" in many Baptist churches, we pray that our denomination returns to its roots of deep-seated, biblical worship.

We have divided the book into two uneven sections (excluding this preface and chapter 1, which provides a basic level overview of some foundational biblical principles governing worship). The first section is the largest part of the

---

1 John F. MacArthur, Jr., "How Shall We Then Worship?" in John H. Armstrong, ed., *The Coming Evangelical Crisis* (Chicago: Moody, 1996), 176.

book. There, we look broadly at the woefully neglected but vitally important doctrine of worship, the regulative principle of worship.

Briefly stated, the regulative principle teaches that God has set forth in Scripture the only acceptable ways of worshiping him and that it is a sin to attempt to worship him in any other way. The opposite view, the normative principle, teaches that we may worship in whatever way we wish as long as it is not forbidden in Scripture.

The regulative principle is perhaps the most unrecognized doctrine in the church today, yet it is perhaps the most vital doctrine of all pertaining to worship. It is important because it provides the construct for examining each and every worship practice and determining whether a specific practice is biblical or not. Yet despite its importance, most Baptists have never heard of it. Fewer still understand it is the foundational theological principle undergirding why we are even Baptists to begin with.

In chapter 2, we offer a full-orbed definition of the regulative principle, and in chapter 3, we defend our definition biblically and examine what we believe to be the elements of proper worship as found in Scripture. In chapter 4, we give a brief perspective on how the regulative principle has been applied in church history, including our own Baptist heritage.

To give the reader a preliminary peek at what we have to say in this section of the book, in a nutshell, we conclude that the regulative principle properly teaches that our worship practices should consist only of what God commands. By confining worship to what is prescribed in Scripture, our churches can avoid many of the difficult questions causing discord in contemporary Christianity. At the same time, we believe an overly stringent application of the regulative principle has caused almost as many problems as its rejection. While we deeply respect those who do not sing uninspired hymns in worship services or who do not use musical instruments in worship, we do not believe the regulative principle stretches that far.

The regulative principle is not a coatrack on which every aspect, circumstance, and mode of worship must be hung in order to be approved. Rather (to change the analogy), we believe it is a hedge that acts as a boundary around broadly prescribed areas of worship. Outside its boundaries, we should not and cannot go. Yet within its boundaries, there is ample room for variation in worship style and practice.

In chapter 5, a bridge chapter between the first and second sections of the book, we seek to apply the learning of the first part to one specific worship practice—what we call the "invitation system." The predominant feature of the invitation system is the post-sermonic altar call—the practice of inviting an inquirer to walk down the aisle of the church worship center and "come forward" to "accept Christ" as the inquirer's "personal Savior." The invitation system, however, goes beyond the altar call and also consists of the practices of praying the "sinner's prayer" and offering immediate assurance of salvation to the one who has come forward and prayed. The invitation system has become so entrenched in most Baptist churches that it has only half-jokingly been called a Baptist sacrament. Our conclusion, in brief, is that the altar call as practiced in most Baptist churches is unscriptural and a violation of the regulative principle.

This does not end the inquiry, however. Not by a long shot. Most people in the pews of even reforming Baptist churches are wholly unprepared to give up entirely their beloved altar call. Although each church situation must be evaluated individually, we venture that it will frequently be impracticable and imprudent for a reforming pastor to simply uproot the altar call without warning and without explanation. This is where the subjects of Christian liberty and accommodation come in, the topics of discussion in the second part of the book. Accommodation is part and parcel of the concept of Christian liberty, which is discussed in bird's-eye fashion in chapter 6. In chapter 7, we turn to a biblical examination of the important but often overlooked practice of accommodation. Finally, in chapter 8, we attempt to briefly apply this practice to the invitation system, concluding that the objectionable aspects of the altar call can be removed, making it appropriate to use the technique in a modified fashion in a reforming situation without violating the regulative principle.

Our conclusions are sure to generate controversy. Why are we tackling this lightning-rod topic? It is not because the authors of the book like controversy. Actually, we don't; we loathe it. Yet we love the truth, for it is the truth, as our Lord told us, that will set people free. Many are involved in attempts to revitalize evangelical Christianity and bring it back to its reformational roots.[2] Many are returning to the doctrinal grounding of conservative Christianity—that is, the evangelical Calvinism held by most early Baptists and Southern Baptist founders. For these things, we rejoice. Yet, in this effort, we must not be content with doctrinal orthodoxy! We must preach and pray and work for the practical

2 For a brief summary of Southern Baptist reformation work, see Ernest C. Reisinger & D. Matthew Allen, *A Quiet Revolution* (Cape Coral, FL: Founders, 2000).

reformation of our churches as well. A doctrinal root must produce practical fruit!

Inevitably, as pastors and other leaders shepherd their congregations into doctrinal reformation, many questions about how to worship will arise. The practical implications of the regulative principle will have to be grappled with. We hope this book will shed some light on these issues by calling for a return to the regulative principle of worship, suitably tempered by the application of common sense and heaping doses of accommodation. It is our sincere desire to encourage local churches, and we hope the thoughts that follow will be useful to pastors and other leaders in the process of reformation. True reformation is a humbling process, but it also creates a new desire to please God and keep his Word. It delivers us from an inordinate desire to defend traditions for which there is no scriptural warrant and, therefore, enables us to approach, in a new way, church issues that have divided us, and with a new concern to be united with all those who love the truth.

The authors of this book do not claim to have all the answers to many difficult worship questions. We are certainly not experts on issues of church music, which are touched on lightly in these pages. We must be cautious and humble as we tread on holy ground. We must guard against the possibility that our own traditions and preferences are driving our analysis rather than submission to the infallible Word of God. We trust that others will build upon or correct as needed the framework set forth in this book. Our perspective is only as good as the scriptural exegesis on which it is based. With that said, we offer a theology of worship we hope can provide some with a way out of the theological thicket associated with how we should worship.

Therefore, this book is designed to be both theological and experiential. It is theological because we explore the biblical underpinnings of these two significant doctrines for worship: the regulative principle and the practice of accommodation. It is experiential because we apply these doctrines to a specific controversial worship practice—the post-sermonic altar call and related components of the invitation system. Our prayer is that the book is most of all helpful to pastors and other Christian leaders grappling with this difficult issue.

Chapter 1

Foundational Principles

It is as natural for man to worship as it is to breathe. Worship is "the very law of his being, as a creature of God, to love, and honor, and serve his Creator."[1] Everyone worships someone or some thing, whether it is the one true God or an idol made by hands.

Because worship is an inherent, inborn characteristic of man, God prescribes the way we should worship. Paying homage to God is the very end for which man was created and exists. As the answer to the first question of the Westminster Shorter Catechism (as well as Charles Spurgeon's version of the Baptist Catechism) puts it, man's chief end is to glorify God and enjoy him forever. God therefore demands that we worship him, the one true God, rather than false idols. This is the first commandment of the law. "You shall have no other gods before me" (Ex. 20:3).

The second commandment of the law is Exodus 20:4, "You shall not make for yourself a carved image, or any likeness

---

1 James Bannerman, *The Church of Christ* (1869, repr., Edmonton: Still Waters Revival Books, 1991), 1:324.

of anything that is in heaven above, or that is in the earth beneath, or that is in the water under the earth." God not only prescribes *whom* we should worship (himself) but also *how* we should worship. The great sin of Jeroboam, the first king of the northern kingdom of Israel after the rending of Solomon's kingdom into two nations, was not the worship of false gods but the false worship of Yahweh, the one true God, in the form of two golden calves. What was God's judgment on this worship practice? "And this thing became sin to the house of Jeroboam, so as to cut it off and to destroy it from the face of the earth." (1 Kings 13:34). God's pronouncement was that Jeroboam had "done evil above all who were before [him]" (14:9).

Worship should pervade our lives. The late John Murray pointed out that we worship in two ways, generally and specifically.[2] In the general sense, we owe God the whole of life. God is sovereign over his creation. As the Creator, he has the right to do with us as he pleases. Conversely, as created creatures, we owe him our allegiance and devotion in all that we do. Thus, E. C. Dargan observed that the English word *worship* is simply a contraction for "worth-ship" and denotes the giving of suitable honor to whom it is due.[3] We are called on to ascribe worth-ship to our Creator. The psalmist said,

> Ascribe to the LORD the glory due his name;
>   bring an offering, and come into his courts!
> Worship the LORD in the splendor of holiness;
>   tremble before him, all the earth! (Ps. 96:8–9)

---

2 For an elaboration of this distinction, see John Murray, "Worship," in *Collected Writings of John Murray 1: The Claims of Truth* (Carlisle, PA: Banner of Truth, 1976), 165.

3 E.C. Dargan, *The Doctrines of Our Faith* (Nashville: Southern Baptist Convention Sunday School Board, 1905), 171.

The apostle Paul said, "So, whether you eat or drink, or whatever you do, do all to the glory of God" (1 Cor. 10:31). By giving God our lives and living our lives before his face, we engage in worship.

At the same time, we worship in specific or specialized ways. We pray, we give thanks, we read and hear the Word of God, we sing, we take the Lord's Supper. And we do so in different settings. We engage in family worship, private worship (devotional time), and public worship. Each has its different rules and expectations. J. I. Packer seems to have had in mind both our general worship and specific acts of worship when he wrote,

> Worship in the Bible is the due response of rational creatures to the self-revelation of their Creator. It is an honoring and glorifying of God by gratefully offering back to Him all the good gifts, and all the knowledge of His greatness and graciousness, that He has given. It involves praising Him for what He is, thanking Him for what He has done, desiring Him to get Himself more glory by further acts of mercy, judgment, and power, and trusting Him with our concern for our own and others' well-being.[4]

This book focuses on public worship. There is something undeniably different, something undeniably special, something undeniably unique about public worship. In public worship, we gather in an assembly as the body of Christ to worship our Lord, "not neglecting to meet together, as is the habit of some, but encouraging one another, and all the more as you see the Day drawing near" (Heb. 10:25). Gathering

4 J. I. Packer, *Concise Theology* (Wheaton, IL: Tyndale, 1993), 98.

as the body of Christ is important because, as John Murray once said, "it is one of the principal ways of giving expression to the unity of the Spirit in the bond of peace, and to the communion of the saints with one another in the oneness of Christ's body."[5]

Yet, several key questions need to be considered when it comes to public worship.

What Is Public Worship?

The first question before us is, What exactly is worship—more specifically, public worship? To worship is to pay honor, homage, or reverence to another. Nowhere in Scripture is worship actually defined. But when the key biblical words for *worship* are examined, it becomes clear that the central concepts are homage, service, and reverence.[6] It is no surprise, then, that theologian John Frame defines worship as "the work of acknowledging the greatness of our covenant Lord."[7] The principal Old Testament word for *worship*, used ninety-five places, is *shachah*, meaning to "depress," "bow down," or "prostrate." The Old Testament idea is therefore "the reverential attitude of mind or body or both, combined with the more generic notions of religious adoration, obedience, service." The principal New Testament word, used fifty-nine times, is *proskuneo*, meaning to "kiss (the hand or the ground) toward." It is to render homage to someone, whether man, angel, demon, or God.[8]

---

5 Murray, "Worship," 166.

6 D.G. Peterson, "Worship" in *New Dictionary of Biblical Theology* (Downers Grove, IL: IVP, 2000) (reproduced in electronic format in The Essential IVP Reference Collection).

7 John M. Frame, *Worship in Spirit and Truth* (Phillipsburg, NJ: P&R, 1996), 1.

8 Phillip Wendell Crannell, "Worship" *International Standard Bible*

Public worship, then, is the collective exultation of the gathered church. In fact, worship is the primary purpose of the church. A worship service is not merely a gathering of individuals who sing some hymns and hear a sermon together. Rather, it is the corporate expression of the body of Christ. It is a unique and unified offering of adoration and honor to God our Savior.

Why Should We Engage in Public Worship?

So then, why do we participate in public worship? The great nineteenth-century Southern Baptist John Broadus succinctly stated in an 1879 sermon, "Why ought we to worship God? Because it is due to him; and because it is good for us."[9] It is as simple as that. We owe God our worship as a matter of duty. As we have already mentioned, God alone is worthy of our worship. He requires our devotion. He is a jealous God who demands exclusivity in worship. And yet, doing our duty, worship, is good for us. This is because it is only in the worship of God that we can truly find satisfaction. This was the very purpose for which we were made. We are most satisfied when we find our delight in our God.

This means that public worship is God-directed, not self-directed. When we engage in true worship, we should not focus so much on how we feel as we sing and pray and take Communion and listen to the preaching of God's Word. We should not even come to church with the purpose in mind of feeling God's presence. No, our primary purpose in coming is, or at least should be, to corporately express our

---

Encyclopaedia, (Biblesoft: PC Study Bible Electronic Database, 1996).

9 John A. Broadus, *Sermons and Addresses* (Nashville: Sunday School Board of the Southern Baptist Convention, 1886), 4.

adoration to God our Creator and Christ our Savior. John Frame quotes a former pastor as insightfully saying, "When we leave worship, we should first ask, not What did I get out of it? But How did I do in my work of honoring the Lord?"[10]

What Should Our Attitude Be in Public Worship?

Our third question addresses our approach to worship—that is, what kind of attitude should we have in public worship? John Murray suggests that reverence should typify the proper attitude in worship.[11] We think he is right. Too much of what passes for worship on the contemporary scene has lost sight of the requirement that worship should be reverent. There is too much frivolity and familiarity in worship today. To be sure, there is a place in life for laughter. There is a place for humor. But when we worship, *reverence* should be our watchword.

At the same time, worship is active. It is something we do. Therefore, our worship is not to be passive. It is not a spectator event. When we sing, we should sing heartily. When we pray, we should pray actively. When we listen to the preaching of the Word, we should listen with hearts open and minds engaged.

How Should We Engage in Public Worship?

Finally, how should we engage in publish worship? Both substance and form are critical to true worship. Worship is not true worship unless it flows from both a heart of faith

---

10 Frame, *Worship in Spirit and Truth*, 5.

11 Murray, "Worship," 167.

and a heart engaged. Throughout Scripture, God condemns "going through the motions" in worship. The Old Testament prophets repeatedly decried external religion devoid of devotion. Samuel told Saul,

> Has the LORD as great delight in burnt offerings and sacrifices,
> as in obeying the voice of the LORD?
> Behold, to obey is better than sacrifice,
> and to listen than the fat of rams.
> For rebellion is as the sin of divination,
> and presumption is as iniquity and idolatry.
> Because you have rejected the word of the LORD,
> he has also rejected you from being king.
> (1 Sam. 15:22–23)

In Psalm 51, after being confronted with his sin of adultery with Bathsheba and the murder of her husband, Uriah, a contrite and repentant David cries out to God:

> Deliver me from bloodguiltiness, O God,
> O God of my salvation,
> and my tongue will sing aloud of your righteousness.
> O Lord, open my lips,
> and my mouth will declare your praise.
> For you will not delight in sacrifice, or I would give it;
> you will not be pleased with a burnt offering.
> The sacrifices of God are a broken spirit;
> a broken and a contrite heart, O God, you will not despise.
>
> Do good to Zion in your good pleasure;
> build the walls of Jerusalem;
> then you will delight in right sacrifices,

in burnt offering and whole burnt offerings;
then bulls will be offered on your altar. (vv. 14–19)

Proverbs 15:8 says, "The sacrifice of the wicked is an abomination to the LORD, but the prayer of the upright is acceptable to him." Proverbs 21:3 likewise says, "To do righteousness and justice is more acceptable to the LORD than sacrifice." Proverbs 21:27 similarly says, "The sacrifice of the wicked is an abomination; how much more when he brings it with evil intent." In Hosea 6:6, God says, "For I desire mercy, not sacrifice, and acknowledgment of God rather than burnt offerings" (NIV).

Perhaps the strongest example of how God feels about heartless religion is found in Isaiah 1:10–18:

> Hear the word of the LORD,
> you rulers of Sodom;
> listen to the instruction of our God,
> you people of Gomorrah!
> "The multitude of your sacrifices—
> what are they to me?" says the LORD.
> "I have more than enough of burnt offerings,
> of rams and the fat of fattened animals;
> I have no pleasure
> in the blood of bulls and lambs and goats.
> When you come to appear before me,
> who has asked this of you,
> this trampling of my courts?
> Stop bringing meaningless offerings!
> Your incense is detestable to me.
> New Moons, Sabbaths and convocations—
> I cannot bear your evil assemblies.
> Your New Moon feasts and your appointed festivals

> I hate with all my being.
> They have become a burden to me;
> I am weary of bearing them.
> When you spread out your hands in prayer,
> I hide my eyes from you;
> even if you offer many prayers,
> I am not listening.
>
> Your hands are full of blood!
>
> Wash and make yourselves clean.
> Take your evil deeds out of my sight;
> stop doing wrong.
> Learn to do right; seek justice.
> Defend the oppressed.
> Take up the cause of the fatherless;
> plead the case of the widow.
>
> "Come now, let us settle the matter," says the Lord.
> "Though your sins are like scarlet,
> they shall be as white as snow;
> though they are red as crimson,
> they shall be like wool. (NIV)

The point of these verses is not that, during the Old Testament period, the sacrificial system was to be ignored or abolished before its time. The point is a more basic one, that the form of religion apart from "heart circumcision"—a regenerated heart, a justified soul, and a life of faith—is empty and meaningless.

Jesus also spoke against vain repetitions and the emphasis on the externals of religion exhibited by the Pharisees of his day. In Matthew 9:13, he said (quoting 1 Sam. 15:22): "Go and learn what this means: 'I desire mercy, and not sacrifice.' For I came not to call the righteous, but sinners."

There is no question about it; God demands heart worship.

Yet, at the same time, form cannot be ignored. The same God who condemned the Old Testament sacrifices of the wicked instituted the sacrificial system in the first place as the authorized form of Old Testament worship. The same Jesus who overturned the tables of the moneychangers in the temple instituted temple worship in his preincarnate state, and he, of course, faithfully worshiped in the temple during his time on earth. The same Jesus who condemned the hypocritical and self-righteous prayer of the Pharisee and praised the humble and genuine prayer for mercy of the tax collector prayed himself and taught his disciples how to pray. We must, therefore, conclude that God cares about the form of worship. As Monte Wilson well said, "The form pointed the worshiper in the right direction; it ensured that all spoke with one heart, one mind, and one voice. . . . We are humans. Not being wholly spirit, we need external aids to lead and support us in our quest for obedient, spiritual worship."[12] This is true in both the Old and New Testament dispensations.

Although this book is primarily about the forms of worship—and the forms God prescribes—it would never do for any of us to ignore the heart. God demands worship in spirit and truth. He demands worship grounded in faith. Irrespective of the form, no one who worships does so faithfully unless he is born again. This principle is paramount over all.

---

12 Monte E. Wilson, "Church-o-Rama or Corporate Worship" in John H. Armstrong, ed., *The Compromised Church* (Wheaton: Crossway, 1998), 71–72.

THE REGULATIVE PRINCIPLE

PART A: DOCTRINE

Chapter 2

The Regulative Principle Defined

It is important at the outset to carefully define the regulative principle with a certain degree of precision. We can do no better in this respect than to call on the formulation set forth in chapter 22, section 1 of the 1689 Baptist Confession: "But the acceptable way of worshipping the true God is instituted by himself, and so limited by his own revealed will, that he may not be worshiped according to the imaginations and devices of men, or the suggestions of Satan, under any visible representation, or any other way not prescribed in the Holy Scripture."[1]

A. A. Hodge commented on the substantially identically worded section of the Westminster Confession of Faith (21:1): "God in his Word has prescribed for us how we may worship him acceptably; and that it is an offense to him and a sin in us either to neglect to worship and serve him in the way prescribed, or to attempt to serve him in any way not

1 All citations to the Baptist Confession of Faith of 1689 are taken from Sam Waldron, *Exposition of the 1689 Confession* (Durham, England: Evangelical Press, 1995).

prescribed." He added, "We have in no case any right, upon the ground of taste, fashion, or expediency, to go beyond the clear warrant of Scripture."[2]

John L. Girardeau's definition is straightforward: "A divine warrant is necessary for every element of doctrine, government and worship in the church; that is, whatsoever in these spheres is not commanded in the Scriptures, either expressly or by good and necessary consequence from their statements, is forbidden."[3] G. I. Williamson put it even more succinctly: "What is commanded is right, and what is not commanded is wrong."[4] Thus, under the regulative principle, true worship is only that which is commanded. False worship is anything other than what is commanded.

The regulative principle flows from the fact that humanity's ability to approach God was barred as a consequence of the fall and that it was impossible for man on his own to renew the fellowship he had enjoyed with God in the garden. Thus, the way of communion with God could be opened again only by God's determination. Not only that, but the very terms of a renewed communion, intercourse, and fellowship with God can be determined by God and God alone.

Contrast with the Normative Principle

Not everyone agrees with the idea that we must confine our worship only to what is commanded in Scripture. Martin

---

2 A.A. Hodge, *The Confession of Faith* (Carlisle, PA: Banner of Truth, 1992), 270, 272.

3 John L. Girardeau, *Instrumental Music in the Public Worship of the Church* (1888, repr. Still Water Revival Books, Edmonton, Alberta, n.d.), 9.

4 Quoted in Waldron, *Exposition of the 1689 Confession*, 268.

Luther did not agree. On January 22, 1531, he wrote to John Gutel, a preacher in Gottingen, concerning certain religious rites not expressly authorized by Scripture:

> I beseech you, further Christ's cause, and introduce no innovations into the services, if in accordance with your views. For the common man gladly seizes any such pretext for damaging God's Word. For although such ceremonials do not promote holiness, still they arrest the attention of coarser natures. I speak chiefly of the rites connected with the mass, altars, etc., and of vestments, torches, and suchlike trifles, which can be retained, if not already done away with, as in Wittenberg. If so, restore them gradually, but let God's Word have the first place, so that no one's conscience may be offended. For they are useful for children and feeble folks, who must be considered.[5]

Notice Luther's instruction here. He tells Gutel that human innovations not commanded by God, such as rites connected with the Mass and the use of vestments, torches, and "suchlike trifles," lawfully can be retained in the worship service because they serve the useful purpose of "arrest[ing] the attention of coarser natures." Thus, if those innovations have been abolished, in Luther's view, they should be restored, albeit gradually, so that no one's conscience may be offended. Nevertheless, if Gutel himself does not agree with a suggested worship practice, it should not be introduced into the service. In other words, whether human innovations should be introduced into the worship service is left entirely to the discretion of the minister.

---

5 Martin Luther, *Letters of Martin Luther* (Reformation History Library, Ages Digital Software CD), 293–94.

In a December 4, 1539, letter to the Elector Joachim of Brandenburg, Luther again articulated his position that worship practices not commanded by God are permissible. He wrote of the Catholic sacrament extreme unction: "The carrying of the sacrament to the sick, although continued, must not be imperative or put in print. For it is of human institution, and not God's command, so it can be retained till a better way is found."[6] Although Luther was clearly uncomfortable with the sacrament, he was not willing to abolish it simply because it was "not God's command."

A separate letter to George Buchholzer, provost in Berlin, shows Luther's famed barbed pen as well as an elaboration of his view that worship practices not expressly authorized by Scripture are permissible as a matter of Christian liberty:

> You will see from the letters what we think of the form of Church government of your Elector, my most gracious lord. In regard to the things of which you complain, the cowl and surplice in the procession on feast days, and the walking round the churchyard on Sundays and at Easter, etc. etc., this is my advice: If your lord, the Margrave and Elector, allows you to preach the gospel of Christ purely, without man's additions, and permits the sacraments of Baptism and the Lord's Supper according to Christ's appointment, and does not insist upon the worshipping of the saints as mediators and intercessors, and the carrying of the host in the procession, nor upon daily masses for the dead, nor holy water nor responses and songs, Latin and German in the processions, then in God's name go round with them, carrying a silver

6 Luther, 396.

> or gold cross, and cowl or surplice of velvet, silk, or linen. And if one of these be not enough, then put on three, as did Aaron, the High Priest, each one more beautiful than another, from which church vestments in the Papacy are named Ornata. And if your lord the Elector be not satisfied with one procession, then go round seven times, as Joshua went round Jericho with the children of Israel blowing trumpets, and if your lord has any desire let him go on in front, springing and dancing with harps and cymbals, drums and bells, as did David when they brought the ark of the Lord up to Jerusalem. I have no objections to that. For such things, if not abused, neither add to nor take from the gospel, but they must never be regarded as necessary nor made a matter of conscience. As to the elevation of the elements in the Mass, this too is an open question when nothing is added thereto, so in God's name raise them as long as you like. We in Wittenberg had good reasons for making an end of the custom—reasons which may not exist in Berlin. And we shall not again begin it, for it is a free thing and not ordered by God, for God's command alone is necessary.[7]

"Where has Christ commanded us to elevate the host and exhibit it to the people?" Carlstadt had demanded. "And where has Christ forbidden it?" was Luther's reply.[8] This exchange encapsulates the distinction between the regulative and normative principles.

Following Luther's lead, the Lutheran and Anglican

---

7 Luther, 413–14.

8 J. H. Merle D'Aubigne, *History of the Reformation of the Sixteenth Century* (Reformation History Library, Ages Digital Software CD), 1036.

churches historically have not held to the regulative principle. Instead, they have adopted an approach to worship called the *normative principle*. This approach is embodied in the Twentieth Article of the Church of England's Thirty-Nine Articles: "The Church hath power to decree rites or ceremonies and authority in the controversies of the faith." In the words of church historian William Cunningham, these churches "generally held that the church might warrantably introduce innovations into its government and worship, which might seem fitted to be useful, provided it could not be shown that there was anything in Scripture which expressly prohibited or discountenanced them, thus laying the onus probandi, in so far as Scripture is concerned, upon those who opposed the introduction of innovations."[9]

The following quaint illustration perhaps best illustrates the difference between the regulative and the normative principle. Two builders go to build a house. Mr. Anglican follows the normative principle, and Mr. Puritan follows the regulative principle. In building the house, "Mr. Anglican must use the materials of the Word of God, but has no blueprint and may use the other materials. Mr. Puritan must use only materials of the Word of God and has a blueprint."[10]

The key question, of course, is whether the regulative principle or the normative principle is biblically grounded. We will reserve this question until the next chapter. First, we need to look at some important qualifications to the regulative principle.

---

9 William Cunningham, *The Reformers and the Theology of the Reformation* (1862, reprinted Carlisle, PA: Banner of Truth, 1989), 31.

10 Waldron, *Exposition of the 1689 Confession*, 268.

Qualifications to the Regulative Principle

The regulative principle is a carefully nuanced doctrine. To fail to appreciate the nuances is to unduly caricature the doctrine. Several important qualifications to its use need to be understood.

Qualification #1: The regulative principle applies only to church ordinances, church government, and acts of worship and not to the remainder of the Christian life.

Chapter 20, Section 2 of the Westminster Confession of Faith states, "God alone is Lord of the conscience, and hath left it free from the doctrines and commandments of men which are in anything contrary to his word; *or beside it, in matters of faith or worship.*"[11]

John Frame states this about this paragraph:

> By what has been called an "eloquent semicolon," the confession at this point draws a distinction between the sufficiency of God's word for faith and worship and its sufficiency for the rest of human life. Roughly it is this: in the general course of human life, we are subject to Scripture alone as our ultimate authority. And when lesser

---

11 Emphasis added. The parallel section of the Baptist Confession of 1689, chapter 21, section 2, unfortunately is not as precise on this point. It states that "God alone is Lord of the conscience, and hath left it free from the doctrines and commandments of men which are in anything contrary to his Word, or not contained in it." Chapter 22, section 1 (the Confession's articulation of the regulative principle), however, makes clear that the phrase "or not contained in it" refers to matters of faith and worship. Thus, although the Westminster formulation is clearer and, therefore, preferable, there is no doctrinal difference between these parallel provisions of the sister confessions.

> authorities command us to do, say, or believe something contrary to Scripture, we have the right to refuse. But in matters of faith and worship, our liberty from human doctrines is even greater. In those areas, we are free to reject not only what is contrary to Scripture, but also what comes from outside Scripture. We might put the point this way: in most areas of life, we may adopt the principle that "whatever is not forbidden is permitted"; but in faith and worship we must adopt the stricter principle that "whatever is not commanded is forbidden."[12]

We will return to this important distinction at a later point when we examine the doctrine of Christian liberty and the related practice of accommodation. For now, suffice it to say that the regulative principle is cabined to worship only. Advocates of its use recognize that, in every other area of life, Christians are under the liberty of the normative principle. In this sense, the regulative principle is an exception to the doctrine of Christian liberty.

Qualification #2: Under the regulative principle, an explicit command from Scripture is not required to legitimize a worship practice.

Chapter 1, section 6, of the Baptist Confession of 1689 states, "The whole counsel of God, concerning all things necessary for his own glory, man's salvation, faith, and life, is either expressly set down or necessarily contained in the Holy Scripture, unto which nothing at any time is to be added, whether by new revelation of the Spirit, or traditions

---

12 John Frame, "Some Questions About the Regulative Principle," *Westminster Theological Journal* 54:2 (Fall, 1992), 358.

of men." The phrase "or necessarily contained in the Holy Scripture" is a clarification of the phrase in the Westminster Confession: "or by good and necessary consequence may be deduced from Scripture." The point is that what "may be by sound logic deduced from Scripture" has the authority of Scripture itself.[13] Hence, as long as an act of worship legitimately may be inferred from Scripture, its use will not violate the regulative principle.

Qualification #3: The regulative principle applies to "things" or "elements" of worship but not to "circumstances" of worship.

To quote chapter 1 section 6 of the Baptist Confession of 1689 again, "There are some circumstances concerning the worship of God and government of the Church, common to human actions and societies, which are to be ordered by the light of nature and Christian prudence, according to the general rules of the word, which are always to be observed."

What is the difference between a "circumstance" and a "thing" or "element" of worship? Circumstances surround worship but do not actually involve worship. Samuel Rutherford called them "adjuncts" of worship. They might include the time and place of worship, the shape of a building, or the use of pews when worshiping.

Qualification #4: The regulative principle does not apply to the "mode" of worship.

Although Scripture clearly prescribes the elements of worship, it does not always detail how those elements are to be

13 Waldron, *A Modern Exposition of the 1689 Baptist Confession of Faith*, 42–43.

carried out. Thus, Frame says, "Preaching is an element of worship, let us say, but Scripture does not specify how many sermons there must be in a service, whether there should be only one preacher or several, how loud or softly one should preach, what text a preacher should use on a particular occasion, etc."[14] As we will see, proponents of the regulative principle have not always kept this last qualification in mind as they have sought to apply the principle to specific worship practices. These qualifications keep the application of the regulative principle from becoming legalistic and stifling. Their importance will be demonstrated as we apply the regulative principle to the invitation system in a later chapter.

Finally, although this is not a qualification to the regulative principle itself, there is one important attitude necessary to the discussion of the regulative principle—humility. There are good and godly men who have adopted the normative principle, as the above quotations from Martin Luther demonstrate, and we must be charitable in disagreeing with them. Many proponents of the regulative principle, in our estimation, have failed at this point. Charitable Christians should disavow statements such as the following by one proponent of an ultra-strict version of the regulative principle:

> All worship by unwarranted means, and all dishonest use of authorized means, would seem to be included in false worship, and may be designated devil worship, for all beast worship is devil worship. The true God is not, and cannot be worshiped with false worship; and as there are but two objects of worship, God and the Devil, it necessarily follows that all worship offered, and

14 Frame, "Some Questions," 359.

> not approved and accepted by the true God—is Devil worship.[15]

Did Martin Luther engage in devil worship? Did all the martyred Anglican bishops (Latimer, Ridley, Cranmer, and others) engage in worship of the devil? Are all who use the Lord's Prayer, the Apostles' Creed, or even the reading of the Ten Commandments as part of their worship of the devil? Do all who sing the hymns of Watts and Wesley and Newton in corporate worship venerate the devil? To ask these questions is to answer them. To say that our Lutheran, Anglican, and yes, Southern Baptist brothers who practice the normative principle engage in "devil worship" is uncharitable, unhelpful, and untrue. While we may seek to persuade them to modify their practice, our goal in this, as in every discussion, is to endeavor to speak the truth in love.

---

15 Quoted from a flier entitled "Error Always Dangerous" distributed by Still Waters Revival Books. Although we appreciate and have personally profited from the ministry of Still Waters Revival Books, and we applaud their mission to make available—and affordable—quality books that would otherwise be out of reach of most people, we cannot agree with their approach to this issue.

Chapter 3

The Regulative Principle Defended

In this chapter, we seek to defend the regulative principle from the vantage point of Scripture. Our first goal is to examine whether the regulative principle itself is scriptural—in other words, to determine whether Christians are limited in worship to what is commanded, either explicitly or by reasonable inference. We will then turn to a determination of what elements of worship are commanded.

As we examine the validity of the regulative principle, one preliminary observation must be made. Scriptural data supporting the regulative principle does not have to be direct to be true. Scripture can indirectly support something and it be just as true as if there were direct evidence. The existence of the Trinity is a case in point. The word "trinity" itself cannot be located in Scripture. Yet there is clear biblical support for the concept of the Trinity, and it is good and proper that belief in the Trinity is a foundational precept of orthodoxy.

The same can be true for the regulative principle. Cunningham states in this regard that the Scriptural evidence of the truth of the regulative principle is not "direct, explicit and overwhelming." We rather think it is direct and explicit, albeit not overwhelming. Of course, all it takes is one verse to make it true. Cunningham also opines that the evidence supporting the regulative principle is "not of a kind likely to satisfy the course, material, literalists, who can see nothing in the Bible but what is asserted in express terms."[1]

Cunningham's language is perhaps injudicious, but his point is nonetheless valid. The evidence supporting the regulative principle is not subject to simple proof-texting. On the contrary, it is woven into the warp and woof, the very fabric, of Scripture. The evidence certainly is "amply sufficient to convince those who, without any prejudice against it, are ready to submit their minds to the fair impression of what Scripture seems to have been intended to teach."[2]

Three Biblical Arguments for the Use of the Regulative Principle

We see three basic arguments from Scripture that support the adoption of the regulative principle, as opposed to the normative principle, in worship.

Argument #1: The sufficiency of Scripture demands the adoption of the regulative principle.

The first argument is that the sufficiency of Scripture demands it. The Bible contains both positive and negative statements declaring the sufficiency of Scripture in areas of doctrine, church government, and worship. On the positive

1 Cunningham, *The Reformers and the Theology of the Reformation*, 33.

2 Cunningham.

side, 2 Timothy 3:15–17 states of the Holy Scriptures that they "are able to make you wise for salvation through faith in Christ Jesus" and that "all Scripture is God-breathed and is useful for teaching, rebuking, correcting and training in righteousness, so that the servant of God may be thoroughly equipped for every good work" (NIV). Second Peter 1:3 states, "His divine power has given us everything we need for a godly life through our knowledge of him who called us by his own glory and goodness" (NIV).

On the negative side, the Bible contains several solemn statements declaring that to introduce any devices and inventions of our own into the doctrine, government, or worship of God is to impermissibly add to the words of God. Proverbs 30:5–6 says, "Every word of God is flawless; he is a shield to those who take refuge in him. Do not add to his words, or he will rebuke you and prove you a liar" (NIV). Deuteronomy 4:2 says, "Do not add to what I command you and do not subtract from it, but keep the commands of the LORD your God that I give you" (NIV). Revelation 22:18–19 states, "I warn everyone who hears the words of the prophecy of this scroll: If anyone adds anything to them, God will add to him the plagues described in this scroll. And if anyone takes words away from this scroll of prophecy, God will take away from that person any share in the tree of life and in the Holy City, which are described in this scroll" (NIV).

From these passages comes the doctrine that the Bible is the only infallible rule of faith and practice and that the Bible alone is sufficient. This idea of the "sufficiency of Scripture" was one of the principal doctrines recovered during the Protestant reformation. Under the battle cry "sola Scriptura!" (Scripture alone), the Reformers fought vigorously for Scripture alone, over and against the traditions of men, pronouncements of church councils, and declarations of popes, to serve as the sole authority in areas of faith and practice.

Throughout their history, Baptists have been strong defenders of this doctrine. As eighteenth-century English Baptist John Gill emphatically declared, Scripture is "the only rule of faith and practice." It contains "the whole of God's will and pleasure toward us." The first American Baptists also vigorously upheld the notion of the sufficiency of Scripture. Roger Williams said that the Bible is the "square rule" that determines "all knowledge of God and of ourselves." And Southern Baptists have been no less vigilant in advocating this doctrine. John Broadus wrote, "What authority has the Bible for us? The Bible is our only and all-sufficient rule of faith and practice." An introductory statement to the 1925 *Southern Baptist Faith and Message* likewise declared, "That the sole authority for faith and practice among Baptists is the Scriptures of the Old and New Testaments."[3]

It invariably follows from this bedrock doctrine that every part of divine worship must be authorized in the Scriptures. Otherwise, how could the "sole authority" for religious "practice" be the Bible? Only the regulative principle teaches that the sole authority for practice is Scripture. The normative principle teaches the opposite, that the authority for practice is the Bible plus the inventions of men not otherwise forbidden in Scripture. Accordingly, the sufficiency of Scripture demands the acceptance of the regulative principle.

---

3 Quoted in L. Russ Bush and Tom J. Nettles, *Baptists and the Bible* (Chicago: Moody, 1980), 105, 107, 78, 225, 387.

Argument #2: The second commandment requires the adoption of the regulative principle.

The second argument in favor of the use of the regulative principle is that the second commandment demands it. Exodus 20:4–6 reads,

> You shall not make for yourself an image in the form of anything in heaven above or on the earth beneath or in the waters below. You shall not bow down to them or worship them; for I, the LORD your God, am a jealous God, punishing the children for the sin of the parents to the third and fourth generation of those who hate me, but showing love to a thousand generations of those who love me and keep my commandments. (NIV)

According to the answer to Question 55 of the Baptist Catechism, the second commandment requires "the receiving, observing, and keeping pure and entire, all such religious worship and ordinances, as God hath appointed in His word." According to the answer to the next question, the second commandment also prohibits "the worshiping of God by images . . . or any other way not appointed in His word."

The answer to Question 109 of the Westminster Larger Catechism expounds on this point: sins forbidden by the second commandment are "all devising, counseling, commanding, using, and any wise approving, any religious worship not instituted by God himself, . . . all superstitious devices, corrupting the worship of God, adding to it, or taking from it, whether invented and taken up of ourselves, or received by tradition from others, though under the title of antiquity, custom, devotion, good intent, or any other pretense whatsoever . . . hindering, and opposing the worship and ordinances which God hath appointed." In other words, it is God's prerogative, and his alone, to ordain the way in which he will be worshiped.

In *The Institutes of the Christian Religion*, John Calvin said that, in the first commandment, God declared himself to be the one true God, apart from whom no other gods are to be imagined or had. In this second commandment, according to Calvin, God declared more openly what sort of God he is and "with what kind of worship he should be honored, lest we dare attribute anything carnal to him." He "wholly calls us back and withdraws us from petty carnal observations, which our stupid minds, crassly conceiving of God, are wont to devise." Then he "makes us conform to his lawful worship, that is, a spiritual worship established by himself."[4] In his commentary on the second commandment, Calvin adds, "The sum is, that the worship of God must be spiritual, in order that it may correspond with His nature. For although Moses only speaks of idolatry, yet there is no doubt but that by synecdoche, as in all the rest of the Law, he condemns all fictitious services which men in their ingenuity have invented.[5]

Thus, the second commandment confirms that it is the prerogative of God alone to determine the terms on which sinners may approach him in worship. This is part of the moral law that Jesus said in Matthew 5 would never pass

---

4 John Calvin, *The Institutes of the Christian Religion*, edited by John T. McNeill (Philadelphia, PA: The Westminster Press, 1960), 383.

5 John Calvin, *Commentaries on the Four Last Books of Moses, vol. 1* (Ages Digital Library, *The John Calvin Collection* CD-ROM), n.p. (comment on Ex. 20:4). A synecdoche is a figure of speech by which a part is put for the whole. *The American College Dictionary*, Clarence L. Barnhart, ed. (New York: Harper & Bros., 1953), s.v. "synecdoche."

away. It is binding on Old and New Testament believers. In other words, it is binding on us.

Argument #3: The regulative principle is affirmed throughout the fabric of Scripture.

The third argument in favor of the regulative principle is that the idea of worshiping only as God has commanded is positively expressed throughout the fabric of Scripture.

The Regulative Principle in the Pre-Mosaic Dispensation

As best we can tell, worship before the Mosaic period was comparatively simple. The requirements were few. Yet it appears that chief among them was the animal sacrifice. God himself may well have instituted this when he clothed Adam and Eve with the skins of animals in the garden after sin entered the world (Gen. 3:21). Nevertheless, we begin with Genesis 4, where we read of the worship of Cain and Abel:

> In the course of time Cain brought some of the fruits of the soil as an offering to the Lord. And Abel also brought an offering—fat portions from some of the firstborn of his flock. The Lord looked with favor on Abel and his offering, but on Cain and his offering he did not look with favor. So Cain was very angry, and his face was downcast.
>
> Then the Lord said to Cain, "Why are you angry? Why is your face downcast? If you do what is right, will you not be accepted? But if you do not do what is right, sin is crouching at your door; it desires to have you, but you must rule over it." (Gen. 4:3–7 NIV)

God rejected Cain's worship, but Abel's worship was accepted. Why was Cain's offering rejected? Three answers are typically given to this question:

1. Some commentators believe it was because Cain presented his offering with a rebellious attitude or merely obeyed an external command with a hypocritical heart. This is undoubtedly true, but it is equally true that, at least in part, the Lord rejected Cain's offering because there was a vital difference between the objective content of the two offerings. Abel offered an acceptable sacrifice "by faith" (Heb. 11:4), and Cain did not.

2. Other commentators (e.g., Calvin, Gill, Girardeau) believe that Cain's sacrifice was rejected because it did not involve the shedding of blood. It may be that God had directly revealed to Cain and Abel that an acceptable offering involved an animal sacrifice—as an object lesson that the Messiah's offering will be by blood as well. Perhaps they had learned this truth from their parents. Either way, John Gill commented on this passage:

> The superior excellency of Abel's sacrifice to Cain's, lay both in the matter, and in the manner of it; the one was offered heartily to the Lord, the other only in show; the one was offered in faith, the other not; Abel looked through his sacrifice to the sacrifice of Christ, not so Cain. Abel's sacrifice was a lamb, a type of Christ, the Lamb of God . . . and the superior excellency of the sacrifice of the one to that of the other, appears from God's regard to the one, and not to the other, (Genesis 4:3–5) from whence it may be observed, that sacrifices were of divine institution, and were very early

> types of Christ; and that there always were two sorts of worshippers, spiritual and carnal ones.[6]

3. Still, a third approach is the suggestion that Cain's offering was rejected because it did not involve the presentation of his first fruits. Whereas Cain brought "some of the fruits of the soil" as his offering, Abel brought "fat portions" from the "firstborn of his flock" (4:3–4). The fat of the animal was considered the choicest part, and throughout the sacrificial system, it was offered to the Lord (e.g., Lev. 3:16). As Wenham states, "the very positive connotations of 'firstlings' and 'fat' in the OT support the view of Keil, Delitzch, Cassuto, Speiser, Kidner, and rabbinic commentators that Abel offered the pick of his flock to the LORD." He continues, "The sacrificial law underlines frequently that only perfect, unblemished animals may be offered in sacrifice (Lev 1:3; 22:20–22, etc.). 'I will not offer burnt offerings to the Lord . . . that cost me nothing' (2 Sam 24:24). Since this is the first account of sacrifice in the OT we might well expect an allusion to this fundamental principle in this story."[7]

Both the second and third approaches are plausible (despite Kidner's view that the second is "precarious").[8] The first approach, on the other hand, in contradistinction to the second and third, ignores the fact that both form and substance of worship matter to God. As the Lord said in

---

6 John Gill, *Exposition of the New Testament* (Exposition of Hebrews) (The Baptist Standard Bearer Electronic Database, 1999), 230.

7 Gordon J. Wenham, *Word Biblical Commentary, Volume 1: Genesis 1–15*, (Dallas: Word, 1998; Nelson Electronic Publisher Database), n.p. (comment on Gen. 4:4, 5).

8 See Derek Kidner, *Genesis*, Tyndale Old Testament Commentaries (Downer's Grove, IL: InterVarsity Press, 1967), 75.

verse 7, "If you do what is right, will you not be accepted?" Abel offered what God was pleased to accept, while Cain did not. Abel worshiped God in the accepted way; Cain did not. In sum, Cain was not willing to limit his way of worship to what God approved.

The Regulative Principle in Tabernacle/Temple Worship

Upon the establishment of the nation of Israel following the exodus from Egypt, detailed directions concerning the way of worship were given in the Mosaic Law. For example, in Exodus 25:40, God instructed Moses to see that every item in the tabernacle was made according to the pattern God showed him on the mountain. In Exodus 31:2–11, God said that the things that went into the tabernacle were constructed by the power of the Spirit of God, with skill, ability, and knowledge in all kinds of crafts. There God says that he gave skills to the craftsmen to make everything as he commanded. Nothing was left to man's innovation.

This was true with respect to the Levitical priesthood too. God prescribed the precise nature of the priests' service, down to minute detail. Yet Aaron's sons Nadab and Abihu varied from the scheme laid down by the Lord and paid a horrible price:

> Now Nadab and Abihu, the sons of Aaron, each took his censer, and put fire in it and laid incense on it and offered unauthorized fire before the LORD, which he had not commanded them. And fire came out from before the LORD and consumed them, and they died before the LORD. Then Moses said to Aaron, "This is what the LORD has said: 'Among those who are near me I will

> be sanctified, and before all the people I will be glorified.'" So Aaron held his peace. (Lev. 10:1–3)

Keil and Delitzch note about this passage that it is not very clear what the offense actually was.[9] The most commonly offered suggestions include (1) penetrating too far into the sanctuary, (2) offering unauthorized coals from outside the temple area, (3) offering incense that did not contain the proper ingredients, and (4) offering incense at the wrong time of the day.[10] Rooker notes that, although the first three of these positions has contextual support, "the immediate context of Leviticus 10 . . . focuses on the nature of the fire itself."[11] In fact, most expositors believe the sin to have consisted in the fact that Nadab and Abihu took the fire for the incense from a private source rather than from the altar fire. Many expositors also conclude that the regulative principle is not in view in this passage because, in taking the fire from a private source, the priests did what was expressly forbidden rather than simply what was not commanded. The NIV translators clearly take this view; that translation states that Nadab and Abihu "offered unauthorized fire before the Lord, contrary to his command."

But Keil and Delitzch point out that the requirement that the source of the fire be the altar "had not yet been commanded by God" and was not commanded until Leviticus 16:12, with regard to the incense offering with which the high priest entered the Most Holy Place on the day of

9 Keil & Delitzch, *Commentary on the Old Testament* (Biblesoft: PC Study Bible Electronic Database), n.p. (comments on Lev. 10:1–3).

10 See Mark F. Rooker, *Leviticus*, The New American Commentary (Broadman & Holman, 2000), 157.

11 Rooker.

atonement. Although we may infer that the altar fire was to be the source for the daily incense offering as well, the point is that no such commandment had yet been given.[12] The better approach, then, is to view the "strange fire" (KJV) as being strange not because it was offered in contravention of God's direct command but because it was not offered in the precise manner prescribed in the law. In fact, this is the approach taken by translators of the NASB, RSV, and NKJV.

Hence, Nadab and Abihu had created "a significant change . . . in the sacrificial rituals," and had allowed something not consecrated by God to intrude upon the ceremony.[13] By their uncommanded act, Aaron's sons "committed such a sin . . . that they were smitten by the fire which came forth from Jehovah, even before their entrance into the holy place, and so died 'before Jehovah.' "[14] As Matthew Henry warned in his commentary, for "it is a dangerous thing, in the service of God, to decline from his own institutions; we have to do with a God who is wise to prescribe his own worship, just to require what he has prescribed, and powerful to revenge what he has not prescribed."[15]

Continuing on, in Numbers 15:37–40, God commanded the people to place blue tassels on the corners of their garments "throughout their generations" (v. 38). This was intended to be a practical and continuing reminder for them: "It shall be a tassel for you to look at and remember all the commandments of the Lord, to do them, not to follow after

---

12 Keil & Delitzch, *Commentary on the Old Testament.*

13 R.K. Harrison, *Leviticus,* Tyndale Old Testament Commentaries (Downer's Grove, IL: InterVarsity Press, 1967), 111.

14 Keil & Delitzch, *Commentary on the Old Testament.*

15 Matthew Henry, *Matthew Henry's Commentary* (Biblesoft: PC Study Bible Electronic Database), n.p. (comments on Lev. 10:1–2).

your own heart and your own eyes, which you are inclined to whore after. So you shall remember and do all my commandments and be holy to your God" (vv. 39–40). The warning that the ancient Israelites not follow after their own hearts and their own eyes is a Hebrew way of describing the "full realm of human cognitive and emotive being."[16] Thus, the admonition is that God's people not substitute their own ideas and inventions for the commandments of God in any respect.

Then, in Deuteronomy 4:2, as the Israelites were about to enter the Promised Land, Moses gave the people final instructions before he died. He warned them not to add to or subtract from the word received from God. In its immediate context, this verse and its injunction refer to the law Moses was about to present to the people. This law, "the gift of God at Horeb," could not be supplemented or reduced in any fashion.[17] Deuteronomy 12:29–32 repeated this warning in the precise context of how God should be worshiped. There Moses said,

> When the LORD your God cuts off before you the nations whom you go in to dispossess, and you dispossess them and dwell in their land, take care that you be not ensnared to follow them, after they have been destroyed before you, and that you do not inquire about their gods, saying, "How do these nations serve their gods?—that I also may do the same." You shall not worship the LORD your God in that way, for every abominable

16 R. Dennis Cole, *Numbers*, The New American Commentary (Nashville: Broadman & Holman, 2000), 256.

17 See Peter C. Craigie, *The Book of Deuteronomy*, New International Commentary on the Old Testament (Grand Rapids: Eerdmans, 1976), 130.

> thing that the LORD hates they have done for their gods, for they even burn their sons and their daughters in the fire to their gods.
>
> Everything that I command you, you shall be careful to do. You shall not add to it or take from it.

Notice that Moses did not simply instruct the people not to follow false gods. He did not instruct them simply to avoid what was prohibited. He told them, "Do not add to" the worship practices God had commanded. Waldron says of this passage, "This clearly implies that it is a great temptation for God's people to see how the world worships and to allow that to have a formative impact on our attitudes about worship. Such an attitude is explicitly forbidden of God's people."[18]

The Regulative Principle in Old Testament Worship Other Than Tabernacle/Temple Worship

Deuteronomy 12:29–32, quoted above, applies to more than simply worship in the tabernacle and later the temple. It provides a broad, general warning to the Israelites, after they had driven out the Canaanite nations and settled in the land, to take care not to follow after foreign gods and adopt pagan worship practices. The added admonition to do all that the Lord had commanded and not add to or take away from the law with respect to worship practices is particularly important in light of the fact that much of Old Testament worship would actually revolve around local Sabbath assemblies and not the temple or tabernacle.

---

18 Waldron, *Exposition of the 1689 Confession*, 270.

Leviticus 23:3 states that the Sabbath is a day of rest and "a holy convocation." Where was this holy convocation to occur? Upon their settlement in Canaan, the Israelites were dispersed throughout the Promised Land, and as the tabernacle was necessarily confined to one spot, it was not accessible to the entire nation except on the occasions of prescribed national feasts. Girardeau queries, "What, then, were they doing on all the other Sabbaths of the year in their cities and towns, villages and rural neighborhoods? It cannot be supposed that on those Sabbaths they never met for worship."[19] Indeed, Leviticus 23:3 says the Sabbath was to be observed "in all your dwelling places." As Keil and Delitzsch commented on this verse, Sabbath observers did not travel to the tabernacle each Sabbath for worship, but "holy meetings for edification were held on the Sabbath in every place in the land, and it was out of this that the synagogues arose."[20]

This practice of gathering in local Sabbath assemblies is confirmed by 2 Kings 4:23. There the Shunammite woman sought to find Elisha when her son had died. When she told her husband she was going to Mount Carmel to find the prophet, her husband, not knowing the plight of his son, wondered why she was going to the man of God since it was not a new moon festival or Sabbath. Keil and Delitzch comment that this verse supports the proposition that "the pious in Israel were accustomed to meet together at the prophets' houses for worship and edification, on those days which were appointed in the law."[21] It is further in accord with advice given to Moses by his father-in-law in Exodus 18:20 that

---

19 John L. Girardeau, *Instrumental Music in the Public Worship of the Church* (1888, reprinted Edmonton, Alberta: Still Waters Revival Books, n.d.), 41–42

20 Keil & Delitzch, *Commentary on the Old Testament*, comments on Lev. 23:3.

21 Keil & Delitzch, comments on 2 Kings 4:23.

Moses (and, by implication, later rulers) teach the Israelites "the statutes and the laws, and make them know the way in which they must walk and what they must do."

Though the origin of the synagogue is shrouded in mystery, it seems reasonable to believe that the synagogue was a natural outgrowth of this already existing practice of meeting together on the Sabbath. Synagogue worship arose during the time of the Babylonian captivity when devout Jews who no longer had a temple in which to worship would gather in a local synagogue to hear the reading of the Law. The typical synagogue service consisted of (1) antiphonal recitations of the Shema (Deut. 6:4) and the Shemone Esreh (a series of praises to God), (2) prayer, (3) the singing of the psalms, (4) readings from the Hebrew law and prophets (interspersed with a Targum—that is, loose oral translation into Aramaic or Greek), (5) a sermon, and (6) a blessing or benediction.[22] The early Christians adopted the synagogue pattern of worship for their churches.

Some supporters of the normative principle suggest that the existence of synagogue worship supports their position because (so they argue) the Bible does not expressly state that God directly appointed synagogue worship. Therefore, they say, it must have been a human invention. Moreover, they suggest, Jesus put his stamp of approval on this human invention by worshiping in synagogues during his time of ministry here on earth.

We respectfully disagree for three reasons. First, it is a fair reading of Leviticus 23:3 to suggest that this is a more than sufficient divine warrant, in the form of an express

---

22 Robert H. Gundry, *A Survey of the New Testament*, 3d ed. (Grand Rapids: Zondervan, 1994), 63.

command, for what became synagogue worship. Second, we do have divine warrant for synagogue worship in the way of biblical example. Jesus worshiped in synagogues every Sabbath, as was his custom (Luke 4:16), and this fact alone takes synagogue worship out of the category of human innovation. Finally, we have divine warrant for the synagogue by way of reasonable inference from Exodus 18:20. The primary purpose of the synagogue was to provide instruction in the Law. Philo called the synagogues "houses of instruction, where the philosophy of the fathers and all manner of virtues were taught."[23] Thus, whether by direct authorization, example, or reasonable inference, we have more than sufficient evidence of divine warrant for synagogue worship. And as we have noted, the invocation of the regulative principle in Deuteronomy 12:32 appears to have application to this local Sabbath worship as well as to the centralized tabernacle/temple worship.

The Regulative Principle in the New Testament

What does the New Testament have to say about the regulative principle? Once again, we see strong support for its adoption. Mark 7:5–13 says:

> And the Pharisees and the scribes asked him, "Why do your disciples not walk according to the tradition of the elders, but eat with defiled hands?" And he said to them, "Well did Isaiah prophesy of you hypocrites, as it is written,
>
> "'This people honors me with their lips,
> but their heart is far from me;

---

23 Quoted in Paul Levertoff, "Synagogue" in *International Standard Bible Encyclopedia* (Biblesoft: PC Study Bible Electronic Database), n.p.

> in vain do they worship me,
> teaching as doctrines the commandments of men.'
>
> You leave the commandment of God and hold to the tradition of men."
>
> And he said to them, "You have a fine way of rejecting the commandment of God in order to establish your tradition! For Moses said, 'Honor your father and your mother'; and, 'Whoever reviles father or mother must surely die.' But you say, 'If a man tells his father or his mother, "Whatever you would have gained from me is Corban"' (that is, given to God)—then you no longer permit him to do anything for his father or mother, thus making void the word of God by your tradition that you have handed down. And many such things you do."

Here the Pharisees criticized Jesus's disciples for failing to wash their hands before eating. This was not hygienic washing to remove germs but a ritual washing that was part of first-century Judaism's oral tradition. Lane says, "The washing was accomplished by pouring water on the hands," and that "a handful of water was required. . . . The position of the hand was cupped, with the fingers flexed to allow the water to pass between them so as to reach all parts of the hand."[24] Jesus responded with a declaration that the Pharisees' defilement was one that ritual hand washing would not resolve. He denounced the Pharisees because they set aside the commands of God to observe their own traditions.

Lane comments that Jesus's sharp rebuttal "sets in radical

24 William L. Lane, *The Gospel According to Mark*, New International Commentary on the New Testament (Grand Rapids: Eerdmans, 1974), 246–47.

opposition the commandments of God and the halakhic formulations of the scribal tradition." The oral tradition was intended to act as a fence, which safeguarded the people from infringing the law. But in reality, "it represented a tampering with the Law which results inevitably in distortion and ossification of the living word of God. The exaggerated reverence with which the scribes and Pharisees regarded the oral law was an expression of false piety supported by human precepts devoid of authority. Jesus categorically rejects the authority of the oral law."[25]

Jesus backed up his charge with a concrete example. He accused the scribes of overthrowing the law—specifically, the application of the fifth commandment that one honors their parents by caring for them in their old age—to honor the scribal tradition associated with the taking of an oath. *Corban* is a technical term in Jewish tradition referring to an offering made to God. The purpose of the formula that had developed by the first century was to place a ban on something, thereby reserving it for sacred use and withdrawing it from common use by another person. In Jesus's illustration, the Pharisees had declared their property "corban" to their parents. This is not to say that the property was promised to the temple. It was simply "off limits" for use by parents in need.

The corban example was simply one of many instances in which the Pharisees' worship was in vain; their teachings were but rules taught by men. This passage teaches with full clarity that human traditions and rules in areas of worship are offensive to God.

J. C. Ryle (an Anglican bishop, no less!) said about this

25 Lane, 246-47.

passage that it "contains a humbling picture of what human nature is capable of doing in religion." It illustrates the dangerous downhill trajectory on which one embarks in introducing the inventions of man into worship: "The first step of the Pharisees was to add their traditions to the Scriptures, as useful supplements. The second was to place them on a level with the Word of God, and give them equal authority. The last was to honor them above the Scripture, and to degrade Scripture from its lawful position. This was the state of things which our Lord found when He was upon earth." Ryle rightly added, "It is just as easy to destroy the authority of God's word by addition as by subtraction, by burying it under man's inventions as by denying its truth. The whole Bible, and nothing but the Bible, must be our rule of faith—nothing added and nothing taken away."[26]

Consider as well Paul's words in Colossians 2:20–23 (NIV):

> Since you died with Christ to the basic principles of this world, why, as though you still belonged to it, do you submit to its rules: "Do not handle! Do not taste! Do not touch!"? These rules, which have to do with things that are all destined to perish with use, are based on merely human commands and teachings. Such regulations indeed have an appearance of wisdom, with their self-imposed worship, their false humility and their harsh treatment of the body, but they lack any value in restraining sensual indulgence.

Thus, Paul warns that things based on human commands and teachings "have an appearance of wisdom, with their

---

26 J.C. Ryle, *Expository Thoughts on Mark* (1857, repr., Carlisle, PA: Banner of Truth, 1994), 139.

self-imposed worship," but they "lack any value" and "are all destined to perish with use." As Adam Clarke put it, "To refuse to receive [God's] teaching in order to prefer our own fancies, is to light a farthing candle as a substitute for the noonday sun."[27] Here again, we have an application of the principle that what is not commanded is forbidden. Colossians 2:23, as much as any other passage, condemns "will worship" (KJV), or worship originating in the human will rather than the mind of God.

Root Causes of Rejection of the Regulative Principle

If the regulative principle has strong biblical support, as we have argued, why is it ignored in most contemporary evangelicalism? There are several possible reasons. One is the lack of fear of God. Waldron states, "Why are men so lenient in their worship? It is because the God of modern men is not a God to be feared. Of all that is not appointed by God in his worship, we must hear Jesus saying, 'Take these things hence!' The child of God will not respond to the regulative principle as if it were an intolerable strait-jacket. He will pray, rather, 'O Lord, teach me to worship you acceptably.'"[28]

Another answer is pride. Calvin put it this way:

> I am not unaware how difficult it is to persuade the world that God rejects and even abominates every thing relating to his worship that is devised by human reason. The delusion on this head is owing to several causes,—"Every one thinks

27 Adam Clarke, *Adam Clarke Commentary* (Biblesoft: PC Study Bible Electronic Database), n.p. (comment on Col. 2:23).

28 Waldron, *Exposition of the 1689 Confession*, 271.

> highly of his own," as the old proverb expresses it. Hence the offspring of our own brain delights us, and besides, as Paul admits, this fictitious worship often presents some show of wisdom. Then, as it has for the most part an external splendor which pleases the eye, it is more agreeable to our carnal nature, than that which alone God requires and approves, but which is less ostentatious. But there is nothing which so blinds the understandings of men, and misleads them in their judgments in this matter, as hypocrisy. For while it is incumbent on true worshippers to give the heart and mind, men are always desirous to invent a mode of serving God of a totally different description, their object being to perform to him certain bodily observances, and keep the mind to themselves."[29]

Waldron put it this way: "Should God decree that he will be worshiped only by those wearing orange shirts and green ties, he would have the right to do so. What arrogance for man to think that he has the least business in determining how God will be worshiped!"[30]

For most people, however, the answer is probably ignorance. Despite its importance, virtually no sermons are ever preached on the regulative principle. Even among those who are theologically minded, serious discussion of the regulative principle has been essentially confined to certain elements of conservative Presbyterianism. Most systematic theologies fail to discuss it at all. Many advocates of the normative principle simply do not know differently. Therefore, one purpose

---

29 John Calvin, *The Necessity of Reforming the Church* (Ages Digital Library, The John Calvin Collection CD-ROM), 218–219.

30 Waldron, *Exposition of the 1689 Confession*, 269.

of this book is to draw attention to the regulative principle in Baptist circles and promote discussion of its application.

The ignorant objector is most often the one contending that the regulative principle is unduly concerned with trivialities involving the mere form of worship and that all God really wants is that his people worship him in spirit and truth. But, of course, to worship God in truth means to worship him in the way in which he wants to be worshiped. Far from being a trivial matter, then, the regulative principle is bound up in God's requirement that sinful man submits to the lordship of a holy God. Simply put, our Creator God and Savior God is entitled to dictate the terms of man's fellowship with him.

We do not doubt that those who advocate the normative principle, like Martin Luther, have wholly good intentions. But we respectfully submit that good intentions are not sufficient justification for avoiding the dictates of Scripture. John Calvin wrote,

> I know how difficult it is to persuade the world that God disapproves of all modes of worship not expressly sanctioned by His Word. The opposite persuasion which cleaves to them, being seated, as it were, in their very bones and marrow, is, that whatever they do has in itself a sufficient sanction, provided it exhibits some kind of zeal for the honor of God. But since God not only regards as fruitless, but also plainly abominates, whatever we undertake from zeal to His worship, if at variance with His command, what do we gain by a contrary course? The words of God are clear and distinct, "Obedience is better than sacrifice." "In vain do they worship me, teaching for doctrines

> the commandments of men," (1 Samuel 15:22; Matthew. 15:9).[31]

Elements of Worship Commanded

We have articulated our view that Scripture supports the regulative principle over the normative principle. But this still does not answer the question of exactly what is commanded in Scripture by way of worship. As John Frame has put it, "the first key to meaningful worship is to do as God commands," but "beyond that . . . there is the question of how best to carry out those commands in our own time and place."[32]

Where should we look to determine what elements of worship are commanded? Some critics of the regulative principle have been quick to point out that certain proponents of the principle have perhaps been overzealous in appealing to proof texts relating to the ceremonial laws of the nation of Israel to justify its adoption. These critics rightly observe that the Old Testament ceremonial law is no longer in force for New Testament believers. Conversely, some advocates of the principle have adopted an unduly cramped view that precludes even the use of musical instruments in church services because the use of musical instruments in the Old Testament was not explicitly confirmed in the New Testament. We believe both these views are erroneous.

The central New Testament passage concerning how we should worship is found in John 4. There, as Jesus spoke to the Samaritan woman at the well, the woman was touched by the convicting power of the Holy Spirit and wanted to change the subject and argue with Jesus about the appropriate

31 Calvin, *The Necessity of Reforming the Church*, 198.

32 John M. Frame, *Worship in Spirit and Truth* (Phillipsburg, NJ: P&R, 1996), xv.

form of worship. "Our fathers worshiped on this mountain, but you say that in Jerusalem is the place where people ought to worship" (John 4:20). Jesus confirmed the validity of the ceremonial law as the appropriate mode of worship for that time. "You worship what you do not know; we worship what we know, for salvation is from the Jews" (v. 22). But undoubtedly to her astonishment, he also foreshadowed the upcoming abolition of the ceremonial law concerning worship. The ceremonies of ritual Judaism had all pointed to the Messiah. Now that he had come in the person of Jesus of Nazareth, there was no longer any need for these rituals: "Woman, believe me, the hour is coming when neither on this mountain nor in Jerusalem will you worship the Father. . . . But the hour is coming, and is now here, when the true worshipers will worship the Father in spirit and truth, for the Father is seeking such people to worship him. God is spirit, and those who worship him must worship in spirit and truth." (vv. 21, 23–24).

This actually was not a new point but was foreshadowed in the Old Testament in Psalm 50:7–23. There, God indicted Israel for not worshiping from the heart:

> "Hear, O my people, and I will speak;
> O Israel, I will testify against you.
> I am God, your God.
> Not for your sacrifices do I rebuke you;
> your burnt offerings are continually before me.
> I will not accept a bull from your house
> or goats from your folds.
> For every beast of the forest is mine,
> the cattle on a thousand hills.
> I know all the birds of the hills,
> and all that moves in the field is mine.

"If I were hungry, I would not tell you,
for the world and its fullness are mine.
Do I eat the flesh of bulls
or drink the blood of goats?
Offer to God a sacrifice of thanksgiving,
and perform your vows to the Most High,
and call upon me in the day of trouble;
I will deliver you, and you shall glorify me."

But to the wicked God says:
"What right have you to recite my statutes
or take my covenant on your lips?
For you hate discipline,
and you cast my words behind you.
If you see a thief, you are pleased with him,
and you keep company with adulterers.

"You give your mouth free rein for evil,
and your tongue frames deceit.
You sit and speak against your brother;
you slander your own mother's son.
These things you have done, and I have been silent;
you thought that I was one like yourself.
But now I rebuke you and lay the charge before you.

"Mark this, then, you who forget God,
lest I tear you apart, and there be none to deliver!
The one who offers thanksgiving as his sacrifice glorifies me;
to one who orders his way rightly
I will show the salvation of God!"

God summons his people to hear him speak. The heavens and the earth are witnesses to what he has to say (v. 4). His address concerned the "meaning and purpose of sacrifices."[33] God first made clear that he did not need sacrifices. Using the language of caricature, he dramatically emphasized that the entire world is his anyway. On the contrary, the essence of worship was not in the sacrifices at all but in thanksgiving, in paying vows to God, in acknowledged dependence on him, and in honoring him (vv. 14–15). The sacrificial system was simply "an avenue through which the worship and thanksgiving of the covenant people could be directed to God."[34] The covenant was the heart of worship.

Keil and Delitzsch have commented on this passage that "what God requires is not by any means the outward worship of sacrifice, but a spiritual offering, the worship of the heart. . . . God desires the thanksgiving of the heart and the performance of that which has been vowed in respect of our moral relationship to Himself and to men." But "it is not the sacrifices offered in a becoming spirit that are contrasted with those offered without the heart . . . but the outward sacrifice appears on the whole to be rejected in comparison with the spiritual sacrifice." In other words, "this entire turning away from the outward form of the legal ceremonial is, in the Old Testament, already a predictive turning towards that worship of God in spirit and in truth which the new covenant makes alone of avail, after the forms of the Law have served as swaddling clothes to the New Testament life which was coming into being in the old covenant."[35]

---

33 Peter C. Craigie, *Word Biblical Commentary, Volume 19: Psalms 1–50*, (Dallas: Word, 1998; Nelson Electronic Publishing Database), n.p., comments on Ps. 50:7.

34 Craigie, comments on Ps. 50:7.

35 Keil & Delitzch, *Commentary on the Old Testament*, comments on Ps. 50:7–15.

All the various elements of Old Testament worship point to Jesus. He is the ultimate sacrifice, ending the need for the offering of bulls and goats (Eph. 5:2; Mark 10:45). He is our great High Priest, ending the need for lesser mediators such as the Levitical priests of the Mosaic system (1 Tim. 2:5). He is God's dwelling among men, the one in whom God tabernacled with his people (John 1:14), ending the need for a physical temple to "house God" (John 2:19–22; Heb. 9:1–5). With the coming of Christ, the ceremonial rituals of Old Testament Judaism were no longer necessary, and with the destruction of Jerusalem and the temple in AD 70, those rituals were abolished.

This does not mean, however, that all Old Testament worship styles are now forbidden and that the New Testament record of the primitive church provides our only model for worship. Those who adhere to a cramped view of the regulative principle make a fundamental hermeneutical error:

> The Puritans made the mistake of not being consistent with their view of covenant theology when it came to their ideas concerning worship. As Ray Sutton has written, in every other area of theological concern they held to the hermeneutical principle that "Unless the New Testament changes it, do what the Old Testament commands." However, when it came to worship, they became dispensationalists and said, basically, "If the New Testament does not command it, we cannot do it." The present-day consequences of this narrowing of the Regulative Principle are asthmatic worship services that only have the one lung of the New Testament to breathe life into

> its services, rather than the two lungs of Old and New Testaments.[36]

In other words, we are free to draw upon the Old Testament and its delineation of elements of worship not specifically abolished as part of the ceremonial law. We can and should draw on both testaments to determine the elements of prescribed worship.

Despite much heated historical discussion about whether certain practices are included in the various elements of prescribed worship, it seems to us that Scripture is relatively clear regarding those elements.

Certainly, prayer is commanded as an element of worship. Philippians 4:6 says, "Do not be anxious about anything, but in everything by prayer and supplication with thanksgiving let your requests be made known to God." Chapter 22, section 3 of the Baptist Confession of 1689 states, "Prayer, with thanksgiving, being one part of natural worship, is by God required of all men. But that it may be accepted, it is to be made in the name of the Son, by the help of the Spirit,

---

36 Monte E. Wilson, "Church-o-Rama or Corporate Worship," 74. To avoid any misunderstanding, we want to emphasize that we do not believe this statement of hermeneutics supports the practice of infant baptism. To the contrary, as will be made clear in the next chapter, we believe the regulative principle, properly construed, stands in opposition to that practice. Fred Malone has well argued in a recent journal article that infant baptism itself violates the regulative principle because the only subjects of baptism that can be conclusively demonstrated from Scripture are professing disciples. Infants are included by our paedobaptist friends only by arguing from purported "good and necessary consequence." Yet the baptism of infants is a normative addition never explicitly commanded nor implicitly suggested in the Bible. See Fred Malone, "Infant Baptism and the Regulative Principle of Worship," *Founders Journal* (Winter 1999): 5–9.

according to his will, with understanding, reverence, humility, fervency, faith, love and perseverance; and, when with others, in a known tongue."

Chapter 22, section 5 of the Baptist Confession of 1689 adds that the reading of God's Word, sound preaching, the hearing of the Word, the singing of psalms, and the receipt of the ordinances of the Lord's Supper and baptism are also to be part of the worship service: "The reading of the Scriptures, preaching and hearing the Word of God, teaching and admonishing one another in psalms, hymns and spiritual songs, singing with grace in our hearts to the Lord, also the administration of baptism, and the Lord's Supper, are all parts of religious worship of God, to be performed in obedience to him, with understanding, faith, reverence and godly fear; moreover, solemn humiliation, with fastings and thanksgivings, upon special occasions, ought to be used in an holy and religious manner."

For each of these acts of worship, we have sound Scriptural support: (1) the reading of Scripture in worship services (Acts 15:21; Rev. 1:3); (2) the sound preaching of the Word of God (2 Tim. 4:2); (3) the hearing of the Word of God (James 1:19); (4) the singing of psalms, hymns, and spiritual songs (Col. 3:16, Eph. 5:19, James 5:13); (5) baptism (Matt. 28:19); and (6) the Lord's Supper (1 Cor. 11:23–34; Acts 2:42).

We can add to the list the collecting of offerings. The New Testament speaks of opportunities to bring gifts for God's purposes and the relief of the poor (Gal. 2:10; 1 Cor. 9:3–12). In 1 Corinthians 16:1–2, Paul instructed the church to collect gifts on the first day of the week, the day the church gathered for collective worship. In Philippians 4:18, he says gifts "are a fragrant offering, a sacrifice acceptable and pleasing to God."

While it is easy to state these elements in their broad sense, as we have done, there is much division over what is encompassed within each element as an appropriate and allowable act of worship. We believe much of this division is unnecessary. Our thesis is that God gives us much freedom within the parameters of these broad categories. God does not give us in Scripture every detail for each element. Rather, his Word supplies us with general rules and categories that are sufficiently elastic for human discretion and common sense to be exercised in the application of them to particular instances of worship. To quote John Frame again, "Scripture leaves many questions open—questions that different churches in different situations can legitimately answer differently. That should not surprise us very much: following God's commands is always the way of freedom. When we substitute human ideas (whether past traditions or contemporary notions) for God's word, the result is bondage to human wisdom. God's yoke, though binding, is much easier and lighter."[37]

A word of caution is in order on this point, however. While there is broad freedom within the boundaries of these categories, that freedom is not boundless. We must take care not to let our God-given freedom swallow up the regulative principle entirely. For example, we must guard against creative redefinition of the elements of worship to smuggle in new and unauthorized practices, such as drama as a form of preaching or dance as a form of praise. This is nothing more than a disguised return to the normative principle.[38]

---

37 Frame, *Worship in Spirit and Truth*, xvi.

38 As the several citations to the works of John Frame suggest, we follow much of his approach to worship and the regulative principle. Nevertheless, it seems to us that he sometimes falls into this trap in his book *Worship in Spirit and Truth*.

Chapter 4

The Regulative Principle in History

In this chapter, we will briefly survey the regulative principle as it has been applied in church history. While the biblical evidence is obviously authoritative, a historical survey is still useful because it can help us understand how the regulative principle has been forged and refined in practical, real-life circumstances. It can also help us see more clearly how to properly apply the regulative principle to current worship practices. As we will see, the historical debate over the particular elements of worship permitted and precluded by the regulative principle well illustrates the twin dangers of both neglecting the principle and miserly applying it.

A Brief Survey of the Regulative Principle in Post-Reformation History

John Calvin is often credited with the formation of the regulative principle. Nevertheless, he did not invent it since, as shown in the last chapter, its origin is found in

Scripture. Calvin did, however, explain and expound it like no one before him. According to Cunningham, the church is indebted to Calvin "for bringing out distinctly, pressing upon general attention, and establishing . . . that it is unwarrantable and unlawful to introduce into the . . . worship of the church anything which has not the positive sanction of Scripture."[1] This forging of the regulative principle should be viewed against the backdrop of the Roman Catholic Church and its elaborate ceremonies and rites that the Reformers denounced and sought to sweep aside.

Calvin distinguished between pure and vitiated worship in his work *The Necessity of Reforming the Church:*

> The rule which distinguishes between pure and vitiated worship is of universal application, in order that we may not adopt any device which seems fit to ourselves, but look to the injunction of Him who alone is entitled to prescribe. Therefore, if we would have Him to approve our worship, this rule, which he everywhere enforces with the utmost strictness, must be carefully observed. For there is a twofold reason why the Lord, in condemning and prohibiting all fictitious worship, requires us to give obedience only to his own voice. First, it tends greatly to establish His authority that we do not follow our own pleasures but depend entirely on his sovereignty; and, secondly, such is our folly, that when we are left at liberty, all we are able to do is to go astray. And then when once we have turned aside from the right path, there is no end to our wanderings, until we get buried under a multitude of superstitions. Justly, therefore,

1 Cunningham, *The Reformers and the Theology of the Reformation*, 27.

> does the Lord, in order to assert his full right of dominion, strictly enjoin what he wishes us to do, and at once reject all human devices which are at variance with his command.[2]

In Calvin's view, "since God has prescribed a certain economy" of worship, it is "presumptuous" to set up another economy contrary to it. He explains, "God in many passages forbids any new worship unsanctioned by his Word; since he declares that he is grievously offended with the presumption which invents such worship, and threatens it with severe punishment, it is clear that the reformation which we have introduced was demanded by a strong necessity."[3]

Calvin applied the regulative principle to preclude the use of religious statues, pictures, and symbols in worship. A number of Catholic innovations in worship were universally rejected. Yet Calvin also applied the newly rediscovered regulative principle to Genevan worship in several ways that we would view today as radical. For example, he discouraged the observance of ecclesiastical festival days such as Christmas and Easter. Although all special days in Geneva had been discontinued before Calvin arrived there, he heartily agreed with the decision.

Calvin also believed that choirs, solo music performances, and the use of musical instruments in public worship were forbidden. Although musical instruments were used (and prescribed) in Old Testament worship, Calvin believed that this "unquestionably formed a part of the training of the law, and of the service of God under that dispensation

2 John Calvin, *The Necessity of Reforming the Church* (Ages Digital Library, *The John Calvin Collection* CD-ROM), 197.

3 Calvin, 218.

of shadows and figures; but they are not now to be used in public thanksgiving. We are not, indeed, forbidden to use, in private, musical instruments, but they are banished out of the churches by the plain command of the Holy Spirit, when Paul, in 1 Corinthians 14:13, lays it down as an invariable rule, that we must praise God, and pray to him only in a known tongue."[4] Yet Calvin's church in Geneva did permit the singing of songs other than the inspired Psalms, including a version of the Ten Commandments, the Apostle's Creed, and the Lord's Prayer.

The Battle for the Regulative Principle in the Church of England

As the Protestant Reformation spread to England, the proper external forms of worship became a prominent battleground between those who sought to radically reform the Church of England along the lines of Calvin's Geneva and those who wanted some reform but also desired that the English church adopt a more mediating position between Rome and Geneva. The more radical Reformers advocated a very restrictive, austere form of worship. Some important reforms were instituted by Archbishop of Canterbury Thomas Cranmer during the reigns of Henry VIII and Edward VI, although not as many as the radical Reformers wished. In the early 1550s, a roaring debate ensued over whether bishops should wear vestments.[5] The issue behind

4 John Calvin, *Calvin's Commentaries, Commentary on the Psalms* (Ages Digital Library, *The John Calvin Collection* CD-ROM), 1:1023.

5 See John Hooper, "The Regulative Principle and Things Indifferent" in Iain Murray, ed., *The Reformation of the Church* (London, Banner of Truth, 1965), 55–58.

the debate was whether the church should adopt the regulative or the normative principle.

All debate ceased in 1553, however, when Mary succeeded Edward VI as ruler of England, and "bloody Mary" instituted fierce persecution against all English Protestants. Many persecuted souls sought sanctuary on the European continent. A congregation of English exiles gathered in Geneva and in 1556 published an order of service called "The Form of Prayers and Ministration of the Sacraments, etc., used in the English congregation at Geneva."

The preface to this "Book of Geneva," as it became known, provides the first statement by an English church that the regulative principle is foundational to the church's government and worship. It states, "For as ceremonies grounded upon God's Word, and approved in the New Testament, are commendable (as the circumstance thereof doth support), so those that man hath invented, though he had never so good occasion thereunto, if they be once abused, import a necessity, hinder God's Word, or be drawn into a superstition, without respect ought to be abolished." Thus, the exiles determined, "we have contented ourselves with that wisdom which we have learned in God's Book, where we be taught to preach the Word of God purely, minister the Sacraments sincerely, and use prayers and other orders thereby approved, to the increase of God's glory, and edification of His holy people."[6]

William Hetherington observes that, upon Elizabeth's ascension to the throne, the Reformation debate picked up where it had left off at the end of the reign of Edward VI. As Queen Elizabeth sought to enforce, for example, the

---

6 "Scripture and the Ordering of Worship" in Hooper, 76–77.

wearing of vestments by Anglican ministers, the emerging Puritan party strongly protested. Arguing from a practical perspective, those who advocated the status quo (the "court party") argued that holding to the external forms of worship common to the Roman Catholic Church would "lead the people more easily to the reception of real doctrinal changes." The Reformers replied that, on the contrary, this "tended to perpetuate in the people their inclination to their former superstitions" and "led them to think there was, after all, little difference between the reformed and the papal Churches."[7]

Hetherington notes that, theologically speaking, the "court party did not admit the Bible to be a standard of Church government and discipline." It affirmed that "things in their own nature indifferent, such as rites, ceremonies, and vestments, might be appointed and made necessary by the command of the civil magistrate; and that then it was the bounden duty of all subjects to obey." In other words, there had to be a standard of uniformity, all right, but that standard was not the Bible but "the queen's supremacy, and the laws of the land."[8]

By contrast, the Reformers, holding to sola Scriptura, believed the Scriptures were to be the standard of church government and discipline as well as doctrine "to the extent, at the very least, that nothing should be imposed, as necessary which was not expressly contained in, or derived from, them by necessary consequence." They "wished to keep close to the Scripture model, and to admit neither office bearers, ceremonies, nor ordinances, but such as were therein appointed or sanctioned" from Scripture. They maintained that "what

7 William Hetherington, *History of the Westminster Assembly of Divines* (Ages Digital Library, *The Master Christian Library*), 32–34.

8 Hetherington, 33–34.

Christ had left indifferent no human laws ought to make necessary; and besides, that such rites and ceremonies as had been abused . . . were no longer indifferent, but were to be rejected as unlawful." In short, the Reformers regarded the Bible as "the only standard."[9]

William Ames

Meanwhile, William Ames, a Puritan exile, carried the theological development of the regulative principle forward in *The Marrow of Theology*. In chapter 8 of that work, "Instituted Worship," he offers a comprehensive examination of the means of worship. Here are some excerpts:

> 2. The means ordained by God are wholly set forth in the second commandment, which forbids all contrary means of worship devised by men under the words, graven image and likeness. Since these were once the chief inventions of men for corrupting the worship of God, they are rightly used for all devices of man's wit pertaining to worship. . . .
>
> 5. Instituted worship is related to natural worship, otherwise it would not be worship, for one cannot give the honor due to God in any way other than by faith, hope and love (so far as the essence of the act is concerned). Thereby, in due subjection, we receive from God what he sets forth for us and with the same subjection we offer all that may be offered to his honor. These acts of offering are themselves performed in a special manner by means which God has instituted for his honor. . . .

9 Hetherington, 34.

> 8. By the command of God instituted worship depends upon and flows from the primary worship of God. This gives the reason and force of those arguments for they are based on the inward and really essential manner of worshiping God, as found in the second commandment . . . .
>
> 10. No instituted worship is lawful unless God is its author and ordainer. . . .
>
> 13. For no one besides God can know what will be acceptable to him and impart that virtue to worship to make it effectual and profitable to us. Nothing can honor God unless it comes from him as the author. Finally, we do not read that the power of ordaining worship at one's pleasure was ever given to any man by God. . . .
>
> 20. That is a most empty distinction which some people make to excuse their additions to worship: "Only corrupting and not conserving additions are forbidden." For every addition as well as every subtraction is a departure from the observance and keeping of the commandments of God, and a corruption of them. Deuteronomy 12:32. . . .
>
> 23. Opposed to instituted worship is will-worship which is devised by men and is unlawful, Matthew 15:9; Colossians. 2:23.[10]

Ames' distinction between "instituted worship" (that commanded by God) and "will-worship" (man-made innovations not founded on Scripture) was adopted by the English

10 William Ames, *The Marrow of Theology* (1629, trans. and repr., Grand Rapids: Baker Book House, 1968), 278–80.

Puritans when it came time to formulate the Westminster Confession of Faith.

The Westminster Divines

In 1637, Puritan George Gillespie wrote a polemic entitled *A Dispute Against the English Popish Ceremonies Obtruded on the Church of Scotland.* In that treatise, Gillespie railed against the "burdensome chain of superfluous and superstitious ceremonies" that were never purged from the English church but were making inroads in the Church of Scotland.[11] Those ceremonies included kneeling in the act of receiving the Lord's Supper, the cross in baptism, the use of bishops, and the observance of Christian holidays. Gillespie denounced these ceremonies in strong language because "the church is forbidden to add anything to the commandments of God which he hath given unto us, concerning his worship and service, Deuteronomy 4:2; 12:32; Proverbs 30:6; therefore she may not lawfully prescribe anything in the works of divine worship, if it be not a mere circumstance belonging to that kind of things which were not determinable by Scripture."[12]

In July 1643, Gillespie and 141 other ministers gathered in London at the command of Parliament to draw up governing documents for the Puritan Church of England. Most of the ministers (or divines, as they were then called) were Presbyterians, but some were Independents or Congregationalists. (None were Baptists). The Westminster Confession of Faith was the last document to be formulated by the Westminster

---

11 George Gillespie, *A Dispute Against the English Popish Ceremonies Obtruded on the Church of Scotland* (Edinburgh: Robert Ogle and Oliver & Boyd, 1660, repr. Edmonton, Alberta: Still Water Revival Books, n.d.), viii.

12 Gillespie, 133.

Assembly, but it defined and still defines the basic doctrine of English reformed Christianity. Paragraph 21, section 2 still defines the regulative principle, stating that God has left the conscience "free from the doctrines and commandments of men, which are, in any thing, contrary to His Word; or beside it, in matters of faith, or worship." This section was adopted by the Westminster divines with virtually no debate. This revealed the near unanimity with which the regulative principle was held in the Puritan churches. Of course, the drafters of the Baptist Confession of 1689 adopted this wording virtually word for word.

At the beginning of the Westminster Assembly, even before the formulation of the famed Confession of Faith, in 1644, the gathered divines had adopted a "Directory for the Publique Worship of God throughout the Three Kingdoms of England, Scotland and Ireland." Although the Public Directory has not been given constitutional status in most Presbyterian churches, the Public Directory provided an indication of how the Puritan divines thought the regulative principle should be implemented. The "ordinary acts of worship" were prayer, the reading of Scripture, the "sound preaching" of the Word, the "conscionable hearing of the Word, in obedience unto God," the "singing of psalms with grace in the heart," and the administration and "worthy receiving of the sacraments."[13] The "occasional acts of worship" were "religious oaths, vows, solemn fastings, and thanksgivings."

Conspicuous by their absence were the offering, the singing of uninspired songs (hymns), and the use of instrumental music. Even the use of "read prayers" (i.e., the Lord's Prayer)

---

13 John Allen Delivunk, "Biblical Authority and the Proof of the Regulative Principle of Worship in the Westminster Confession," *Westminster Theological Journal* 58:2 (Fall 1996): 252.

in worship services was discountenanced, as were the use of the Apostles' Creed in the administration of the sacraments and the habit of the minister to bow in silent prayer upon entering the pulpit. The Scottish office of "reader" was abolished as unwarranted by Scripture. Instead, the public reading of the Word of God was to be conducted by the minister. The Directory also abolished all festival days, including Christmas, and affirmed that "there is no day commanded in Scripture to be kept holy under the Gospel but the Lord's Day, which is the Christian Sabbath.[14]

Looking back, Warfield said about the Directory, "It can scarcely fail to commend itself as an admirable set of agenda, in spirit and matter alike well fitted to direct the public services of a great Church. It is notable for its freedom from petty prescriptions and 'superfluities' and for the emphasis it places upon what is specifically commanded in the Scriptures."[15] Nevertheless, the Directory was generally neglected in England.

The Use of the Regulative Principle among the Baptists

It can be persuasively argued that a more consistent view of the regulative principle led seventeenth-century English Separatists to become Baptists in the first place. The principle recovered in the Protestant Reformation that Scriptural warrant is required for a worship practice to be permitted was applied with full vigor by many Separatists, leading them to

14 Benjamin Breckinridge Warfield, "The Westminster Assembly and its Work," *The Works of Benjamin B. Warfield* (Grand Rapids: Baker Book House, 2000), 6:45–51.

15 Warfield, 51.

reject infant baptism, which is not commanded or otherwise authorized by good and necessary consequence in the Bible, and instead to adopt believers' baptism.

Baptist Adoption of the Regulative Principle

The regulative principle, then, was an important part of early Particular Baptist worship. As we have already seen, the drafters of the Baptist Confession of 1689 (which was actually formulated in 1677) adopted the Westminster Confession's provision regarding the regulative principle with only minor grammatical changes. Similarly, the drafters of the Baptist Catechism, prepared in 1693, drew heavily on the Westminster Shorter Catechism, including its statement that the Second Commandment "forbiddeth the worshipping of God by images . . . or any other way not appointed in his word."[16] Thus, the worship of the seventeenth-century Particular Baptists was virtually identical to that of other Calvinistic denominations. As Horton Davies described them, "baptism apart, it would be difficult to distinguish their worship from that of Independents."[17]

John Gill was a strong though surprisingly inconsistent advocate of the regulative principle. Gill was the most famous eighteenth-century Baptist and pastor of the "Goat Yard" Southwark, London, church (from 1720 to 1771) that Charles Spurgeon would later pastor. Gill was a strong defender of Calvinist orthodoxy, and it was largely his preaching and writing that kept the eighteenth-century Particular Baptists from following their General Baptist brethren down

16 Quoted from Tom J. Nettles, *Teaching Truth, Training Hearts: The Study of Catechisms in Baptist Life* (Amityville, NY: Calvary Press, 1998), 68.

17 Horton Davies, *Worship and Theology in England*, 2:504, quoted in H. Leon McBeth, *The Baptist Heritage* (Nashville: Broadman, 1987), 93.

the road of heresy to Socianism and Unitarianism. The great Anglican hymn writer Augustus Toplady said of him, "Perhaps no man, since the days of St. Austin, has written so largely, in defense of the system of Grace; and certainly, no man has treated that momentous subject, in all its branches, more closely, judiciously, and successfully."[18]

Gill articulated his views on the regulative principle when, in 1751, a Welsh Anglican attempted to have all dissenting children in Wales catechized according to the Thirty-Nine Articles of the Church of England to rid them of Baptist tendencies. Gill sprang to the defense of Welsh Baptists by publishing a pamphlet in both English and Welsh entitled "The Dissenter's Reasons for Separating from the Church of England." In this pamphlet, Gill listed eleven points of disagreement with the established church, several of which were explicitly based on the regulative principle. For example, Gill's fifth point was that the Church of England did not rightly administer the ordinances of baptism and the Lord's Supper. In particular, the "sign of the cross used in baptism is entirely unscriptural, an human invention." In addition, "the introduction of sponsors and sureties, or godfathers and godmothers, is without any foundation from the word of God; it is a device of men." Further still, "the subjects to which it is administered are not the proper ones, namely infants; we do not find in all the word of God, that infants were commanded to be baptized, or that ever any were baptized by John, the first administrator of that ordinance, nor by Christ, nor by his apostles, nor in any of the primitive churches." Gill's sixth point was that the Church of England had offices beyond the scripturally mandated ones of bishop and deacon: "It having

18 Quoted in John Rippon, *Life and Writings of the Rev. John Gill, D.D.* (Harrisonburg, VA: Gano Books, 1992), 137–138.

such ecclesiastical officers and offices in it, which are not to be found in the word of God; and which is another reason why we separate from it." His tenth point was that the Book of Common Prayer was objectionable because, among other reasons, "it directs to the observation of several fasts and festivals, which are no where enjoined in the word of God." Gill stated in his ninth point that Anglican ceremonies were pagan, Jewish, or Catholic. He mentioned bowing to the east and bowing to the altar and bowing when the name of Jesus was mentioned as pieces of superstition and "will worship."[19]

Of other practices such as "particular garments worn by persons in sacred office," he stated,

> And as for such ceremonies which in their own nature are neither good nor bad, but indifferent, they ought to be left as such, and not imposed as necessary; the imposition of things indifferent in divine service as necessary, as if without which it could not be rightly performed, is a sufficient reason why they ought not to be submitted to: such and such particular garments worn by persons in sacred office, considered as indifferent things, may be used or not used; but if the use of these is insisted on, as being holy and necessary, and without which divine worship cannot rightly be performed, then they ought to be rejected as abominable.[20]

This is a somewhat confusing statement. Although Gill here insisted that such ceremonies, which were "neither good nor

19 John Gill, "The Dissenter's Reasons for Separating from the Church of England" in The Collected Writings of John Gill (The Baptist Standard Bearer Electronic Database), 5, 6, 8, 11, 10.

20 Gill, 10.

bad, but indifferent," could not be insisted on as necessary and essential elements of worship, he nonetheless allowed that they could be used in worship if not required. This is an inconsistency in Gill's adoption of the regulative principle, perhaps occasioned by the fact that Gill himself, to the dismay of his Baptist brethren, insisted on wearing a gown adorned with very large bibs as a symbol of his office.[21] Certainly, a deviation on a single point should not detract from his overall support of the regulative principle.

Early American Baptists also adhered to the regulative principle. New England Baptists relied on it as their linchpin argument against infant baptism. Thomas Gould, the first pastor of the first Baptist church in Boston, explained the argument as follows:

> They called me forth to know why I would not bring my child to baptism? My answer was, I did not see any rule of Christ for it, for that ordinance belongs to such as can make profession of their faith, as the Scripture doth plainly hold forth. They answered me, that was meant of grown persons and not of children. But that which was most alleged by them was, that children were capable of circumcision in the time of the law, and therefore as capable in the time of the gospel of baptism; and asked me, why children were not to be baptized in the time of the gospel, as well as children were circumcised in the time of the law? My answer was, God gave a strict command in the law for the circumcision of children; but we have no command in the

21 George Ella, *John Gill and the Cause of God and Truth* (Durham, England: Go, 1995), 127.

> gospel, nor example, for the baptizing of children. . . .
>
> At another meeting, the church required me to bring out my child to baptism. I told them I durst not do it, for I did not see any rule for it in the word of God. They brought many places of Scripture in the Old and New Testament, as circumcision and the promise to Abraham, and that children were holy, and they were disciples. But I told them that all these places made nothing for infant baptism. Then stood up W. D. in the church and said, "Put him in the court! Put him in the court!" But Mr. Sims said, "I pray forbear such words." But it proved so, for presently after they put me in the court, and put me in seven or eight courts.[22]

Gould's argument provoked a fury among the Congregational majority, who practiced infant baptism but who also held dearly to the regulative principle. This is illustrated by the following quotation from the great John Cotton, republished in Benedict's *General History of the Baptist Denomination*, in which Cotton attributes the Baptist argument to Satan:

> Mr. Cotton says, Satan, despairing of success by more powerful arguments, "chooseth rather to play small game, as they say, than lose all. He now pleadeth no other argument in these stirring times of reformation, than may be urged from a main principle of purity and reformation, namely

22 David Benedict, *A General History of the Baptist Denomination* (1813, repr. in Ages Digital Library, Reformation History Library), 1:370, 371.

> that no duty of God's worship, nor any ordinance of religion is to be administered in the church, but such as hath just warrant from the word of God. And in urging this argument against the baptism of children, Satan transformeth himself into an angel of light."[23]

Baptist immigrants from England brought the regulative principle to the Middle Colonies when they carried the 1689 Confession to this country. The Philadelphia Association formally adopted it in 1742, modifying it only slightly and calling it the Philadelphia Confession. American Particular Baptists, called "Regular Baptists," subsequently carried this confession and its incorporation of the regulative principle to Virginia, South Carolina, Tennessee, and other parts of the American South. Tom Nettles has said that the Baptist Catechism, which included the regulative principle, "defined what it was to be a Baptist throughout the eighteenth century, and for some years into the nineteenth."[24]

Even the frontier Separatist Baptists of the Sandy Creek Association, who were seen as more "enthusiastic" in their manner of worship than their Regular Baptist brethren, appear to have held to the regulative principle. In 1774, a union of certain Regular Baptists and Separatist Baptists in Virginia was thwarted, not because one side or the other was insufficiently orthodox in the area of worship but because the Regular Baptists did not measure up to Separatist Baptist requirements in wholly unrelated areas. The Separatist Baptists considered the Regular Baptists to be (1) not sufficiently strict in receiving church members, (2) too

---

23 Benedict, 1:344.

24 Nettles, *Teaching Truth, Training Hearts*, 47.

superfluous in dress, and (3) too careless in receiving into membership persons whose baptism was not on the right side of their salvation![25] In 1787, another group of Separatist and Regular Baptists in Virginia merged with the Separatist Baptists, declaring that a "large majority" of them accepted the Philadelphia Confession.[26]

According to Benedict, the early Separatist Baptists practiced nine Christian rites: "baptism, the Lord's supper, love-feasts, laying on of hands, washing feet, anointing the sick, right hand of fellowship, kiss of charity, and devoting children. ("Devoting children" was essentially a baby dedication ceremony, still practiced in many Baptist churches.) They also held to ruling elders, eldresses, deaconesses, and weekly communion." Aware that many of these rites were controversial, Benedict stated that not all the Sandy Creek churches adopted each of these rites. Nevertheless, he also took pains to point out that each of them "appear[ed] to be suggested by the Scriptures."[27] By 1813, those rites "of a peculiar nature" (including the offices of eldresses and deaconesses) had fallen into disuse.

In the nineteenth century, the regulative principle continued to be honored in many churches that would make up the Southern Baptist Convention. For example, the Baptist Catechism, which explicitly adopted the regulative principle, was widely used in the South through much of that century. Even as late as 1900, Richard Dudley could say in a spirited defense of Baptist beliefs, "I am not a Baptist because Baptists practice restricted communion, or immersion, or refuse

---

25 Benedict, *General History of the Baptist Denomination*, 2:92–93.

26 Robert Baylor Semple, *History of the Baptists in Virginia* (1810, rev. 1894, repr. Lafayette, TN: Church History Research and Archives, 1976), 100.ijo.

27 Benedict, *General History of the Baptist Denomination*, 2:98.

infant baptism. I am a Baptist because by the fundamental principle of Protestantism I am bound by the Word of God in all matters of faith and practice."[28]

William B. Johnson, the first president of the Southern Baptist Convention, preached a sermon on September 22, 1844, at Gilead Meeting House, Union District, South Carolina, which contained the following comments:

> The church is constituted the highest tribunal on this earth in the management of her own affairs. The authority with which she is thus vested, is delegated to her by her great Head, without the liberty of transferring it to any human power. And if she cannot transfer it, no human power can assume it. . . .
>
> The doctrine of the Lord we are commanded to believe, and the precepts that are enjoined we are also commanded to obey. These are all contained in the holy Scriptures.
>
> The judicial and ceremonial commands were peculiar to the Jews and are not binding on Christians. But whatever is moral is of universal obligation, though we are to look more particularly into the New Testament for the laws by which the church and her members are to be governed. To transcribe these laws would too far exceed the limits and design of this discourse. I must take occasion, however, to observe in this place, that the laws, which the Head of the

---

28 R. M. Dudley, "The Distinctive Baptist Way: Our Reasons for the Separate Existence of the Baptists," in *Baptist Why and Why Not*, Timothy and Denise George, eds. (Nashville: Broadman & Holman, 1996), 30.

> church has enacted for his people are binding, and must be obeyed. They are not to be regarded as matters of opinion, or of indifference. We are not at liberty to judge of their propriety, as a reason for obeying or disobeying them, or to explain them away, so that they may be made to suit our convenience. We cannot substitute any others in their place, nor allow any body of men to change them for us.[29]

J. M. Pendleton, a Landmark Baptist whose writings were popular among many Southern Baptists of the nineteenth century, wrote against infant baptism on the ground of the regulative principle. He wrote, "I lay it down as a principle of common sense which commends itself to every unprejudiced mind that a commission to do a thing or things authorizes only the doing of that thing or those things specified in it. The doing of all other things is virtually prohibited." He analogized this "common-sense" principle to the legal maxim *expressio unius est exclusio alterius*—the expression of one thing is the exclusion of another.[30]

John Broadus, one of the founders of Southern Baptist Theological Seminary, appears to have accepted a version of the regulative principle. In a sermon preached at the dedication of the Second Baptist Church in St. Louis, Missouri, in 1879, he criticized the view that anything and everything that

---

29 William Bullein Johnson, "A Church of Christ With Her Officers, Laws, Duties & Form of Government" (a sermon delivered September 22, 1844, at Gilead Meeting House, Union Dist., South Carolina), Founders Ministries, accessed December 13, 2021, https://founders.org/library/a-church-of-christ.

30 J.M. Pendleton, *Three Reasons Why I Am a Baptist With a Fourth Reason Added, On Communion* (Graves, Marks & Rutland, 1856, repr. Buffalo, IO: Stacy Printing Co., 1989), 12.

may at all help as an external expression of devotion to God is permissible. Using pictures and statutes as worship aids, he said, violated the second commandment. Using "secular music in sacred worship" is dangerous. "We must cultivate the power of making [music] a help to religious worship . . . or we must refuse to have it." Thus, "not everything . . . that may promote devotion is to be regularly used" in worship.[31]

Basil Manly Jr. incorporated the principle (albeit in abbreviated form) in the Southern Baptist Theological Seminary's Abstract of Principles. Article XIV, "The Church," states,

> The Lord Jesus is the Head of the Church, which is composed of all his true disciples, and in him is invested supremely all power for government. According to his commandment, Christians are to associate themselves into particular societies or churches; and *to each of these churches he hath given needful authority for administering* that order, discipline and *worship which he hath appointed.*

The Abstract of Principles is still the governing document of Southern Seminary as well as Southeastern Baptist Theological Seminary, and all the professors to those institutions must affirm their agreement with its principles.

Baptist Application of the Regulative Principle

As we have seen, the Baptists of earlier years embraced the regulative principle, although the Baptist formulation of it generally has not been as stringent as the Presbyterian version. The strictest Presbyterian adherents to it, for example, have never accepted hymn singing in worship services apart

31 Broadus, *Sermons and Addresses*, 16–19.

from the Psalms. Some refuse to use musical instruments as an accompaniment to singing. Others forego musical instruments but have a "precentor" use a pitch pipe to get the congregation started on the right key. Most Baptist disputes concerning the application of the regulative principle revolved around attempts to move away from similar positions.

Benjamin Keach, an early Particular Baptist, came to reject the Psalms-only view in the late seventeenth century. Keach was a signatory and adherent to the Baptist Confession of 1689 and, therefore, a proponent of the regulative principle. At the same time, he was the first Baptist to introduce the regular singing of uninspired hymns into the normal worship of an English congregation.[32] Keach first introduced the singing of hymns to his Southwark congregation at the conclusion of the Lord's Supper between 1673 and 1675. He later expanded the practice of singing hymns to thanksgiving services. By 1691, the church had voted to have a hymn sung following the service every Sunday. Keach's son-in-law Thomas Crosby recorded of the practice:

> Though he had very great success therein, yet it brought upon him much trouble and ill-will. When he was convinced that singing the praises of God was an holy ordinance, he laboured earnestly and with a great deal of prudence and caution, to convince his people thereto; and first obtained their consent to the practice of it at the conclusion of the sacrament of the Lord's supper, and had but two of the brethren . . . that opposed him therein. . . . After his church had continued in this practice about six years, they further assented

32 A. C. Underwood, *A History of the English Baptists* (London: The Carey Kingsgate Press Limited, 1956), 112.

> to practice the same on public thanksgiving days, and continued therein about fourteen years; and then by a regular act of the church, in a solemn manner agreed, to sing the praises of God on every Lord's day, excepting about five or six persons that dissented therefrom; and if I am not mistaken, was the first church of the Baptists that practiced this holy ordinance. And so far was Mr. Keach, or the church, from imposing on the consciences of those few that dissented . . . that they agreed to sing when prayer was concluded after the sermon; and if those few who were not satisfied could not stay the time of singing, they might freely go out, and the church would not be offended at them . . . [but the few] drew over some others in the church to join with them, and wrought up their uneasiness to that pitch, that at last a separation ensued; and thereupon another church was founded on the same principles, singing only excepted.[33]

With the publication of Keach's hymnbook in 1691, heated controversy broke out among the Particular Baptists, with highly respected ministers weighing in on both sides. Keach published *The Breach Repaired in God's Worship; or Singing of Psalms, Hymns, and Spiritual Songs, proved to be an Holy Ordinance of Jesus Christ* in 1691 to defend the practice of hymn singing. Holding to the regulative principle as he did, he cited explicit commands of Scripture in support of the practice—Ephesians 5:19, Colossians 3:16, and James 5:13. Because he relied on Scriptural support, Keach could adhere to the regulative principle and at the same time argue that hymn singing was quite permissible so long as the hymns

33 Quoted in Underwood, 132–33.

sung were "absolutely congruous" to God's Word. Other early Particular Baptists agreed with Keach that the regulative principle did not preclude the use of hymns and congregational singing. Vavasor Powell (1617–1670) declared that the singing of psalms, hymns, and spiritual songs "is a continued Gospel-ordinance and duty; and to be performed by all, but especially in the Churches." In 1680, Hercules Collins published *An Orthodox Catechism*, which contained an appendix "concerning the Ordinance of Singing."[34]

When the English Particular Baptists brought the 1689 Confession to America from the mother country and called it the Philadelphia Confession, they added a new chapter 23, which stated that "singing the praises of God, is a holy ordinance of Christ, and not a part of natural religion, or a moral duty only; but that it is brought under divine institution, it being enjoined on the churches of Christ to sing psalms, hymns, and spiritual songs; and that the whole church in their public assemblies, as well as private Christians, ought to (Hebrews 2:12, James 5:13) sing God's praises according to the best light they have received."[35]

By 1813, the controversy over singing in English Baptist churches had essentially withered away, so much so that David Benedict, pastor of the Baptist church in Pawtucket, Rhode Island, and author of a leading history of the Baptists, did not comprehend the theological underpinnings of it. He observed that, by his time, "this controversy was quieted, and the practice of singing was adopted by many churches, which had formerly neglected it, and I conclude now generally

---

34 Michael A.G. Haykin, *Kiffin, Knollys and Keach* (Leeds, England, Carey, 1996), 92–96.

35 Timothy George, *Baptist Confessions, Covenants, and Catechisms* (Nashville: Broadman & Holman, 1996), 82.

prevails." Although some Baptists who emigrated to America in earlier days had "brought over with them from their mother country, a prejudice against singing in public worship, and in some places, especially in Rhode-Island, there have been found, until within a few years past, a few ministers, who would not adopt the practice," Benedict admitted: "I know not what arguments those Baptists brought against singing in public, who omitted the practice." He surmised that the practice originated in times of persecution when Baptists were obliged to hold their meetings in secret and singing might give them away to the persecuting authorities.[36]

The controversies over hymn singing, unfortunately, rent the Particular Baptists and caused them to lose much of their effectiveness. This clearly troubled Keach. He wrote in *The Breach Repaired in God's Worship*, "Lord, give us Moderation; don't let us be bitter against one another."[37] The following bit of verse on the controversy well captures his view:

> Our wounds do stink and are corrupt,
> Hard swellings do we see;
> We want a little ointment, Lord,
> Let us more humble be.[38]

There is a lesson to be learned here by all of us as we consider a twenty-first-century application of the regulative principle.

Parenthetically, modern-day proponents of a less stringent application of the regulative principle do not believe singing is a specific element of worship. For example, John

---

36 Benedict, *A General History of the Baptist Denomination*, 1:201.

37 H. Leon McBeth, *A Sourcebook for Baptist Heritage* (Nashville: Broadman, 1990), 68.

38 Underwood, 133.

Frame says that singing "does not have an independent function in worship; rather, it is a way of doing many different things: praying, teaching, blessing, fellowshipping, etc."[39] Vern Poythress concurs: "We regard teaching by singing and teaching in the narrow sense as simply two forms of teaching, each particularly effective in meeting certain needs and expressing certain aspects of Christian doctrine. Each has its advantages and limitations, due to the nature of the medium of expression. . . . To us they appear little more 'separate' than preaching to a visible audience versus preaching over the radio."[40] Interestingly, the Baptist Confession of 1689 hints at this approach as well, declaring that religious worship consists, among other things, of "teaching and admonishing one another in psalms, hymns and spiritual songs."

John Gill's application of the regulative principle is particularly noteworthy in that it closely mirrors the approach we suggest in this work. Article XII of his Southwark church's Declaration of Faith and Practice (replacing the Baptist Confession of 1689) states, "We also believe, That singing of psalms, hymns, and spiritual songs vocally, is an ordinance of the Gospel, to be performed by believers; but that as to time, place, and manner, every one ought to be left to their liberty in using it."[41] As reflected in this church's confession, Gill viewed the singing of psalms, hymns, and spiritual songs to be "an ordinance of the Gospel." Put differently, singing was considered to be an event of worship subject to the regulative

---

39 Frame, *Worship in Spirit and Truth*, 57.

40 Vern S. Poythress, "Ezra 3, Union With Christ, and Exclusive Psalmody," *Westminster Theological Journal*, vol. 37, no. 1–2 (1974–75), 225–226.

41 "A Declaration of the Faith and Practice of the Church of Christ, in Carter Lane, Southwark, *The Collected Writings of John Gill* (The Baptist Standard Bearer Electronic Database), 5.

principle. Yet "as to time, place and manner, every one ought to be left to their liberty in using it." In other words, there was broad freedom as to how congregational singing was to be done.

This broad freedom was liberally exercised by the Southwark church, which frequently switched back and forth between periods of exclusive psalm singing and hymn singing. Although Gill did not agree with Keach that Ephesians 5:19 and Colossians 3:16 referred to uninspired hymns as well as inspired ones, Gill clearly allowed his congregation to sing uninspired hymns during corporate worship. He accordingly did not view the regulative principle to bar the practice. Yet, at the same time, he was personally ambivalent about the subject. On the one hand, Gill judged uninspired hymns to be "in a good measure, unnecessary, since we are so well provided with a book of psalms and scriptural songs, indited by the Spirit of God, and suitable on all occasions." On the other hand, he observed that "such compositions were made use of very early, even from the time of the Apostles," and, "I deny not but that they may now be useful; tho a great deal of care should be taken that they be agreeable to the sacred writings and the analogy of faith, and that they be expressed, as much as can be, in scriptural language."42 Gill even participated in the publication of a hymnbook, used hymns in his private devotional time, and quoted a verse from Isaac Watts on his deathbed.

The approach adopted by John L. Dagg, the first writing Southern Baptist, also appears to be closely related to the approach we have suggested in this book. Dagg does not

42 John Gill, "A Discourse on Singing of Psalms As Part of Divine Worship," *The Collected Writings of John Gill* (The Baptist Standard Bearer Electronic Database), 5.

mention the regulative principle by name in his *Manual of Church Order*. But he appears to have been a strong proponent of it. In his chapter on public worship, he states that "public worship should include prayers, songs of praise, and the reading and expounding of God's word," the traditional elements of worship under the regulative principle. In his chapter on the "Duty of Baptists," he states that "it is our duty to maintain the ordinances of Christ, and the church order which he has instituted, in strict and scrupulous conformity to the Holy Scriptures." He continues, "When the finger of God points out the way, no place is left to us for human preferences." With respect to human ordinances, he observes that "ecclesiastical organizations" had "corrupted the ceremonies of worship which he instituted." One of the "earliest corruptions of Christianity" was the tendency to "substitute ceremonies of human invention for the ordinances of God." Restoring these ordinances to their original purity (undoubtedly a reference to believer's baptism) was "a service to which God has specially called the Baptists."[43]

Dagg rebutted the charge that the "various forms of religion" are "matters of minor importance" (although he clearly and correctly believed they were subordinate to the moral truths and precepts of God's Word). He responded that we are "bound to obey God in everything," and "no command which he has given can be so unimportant that we are at liberty to disobey it at our pleasure." But when it came time to apply the regulative principle to specific elements of worship, Dagg clearly accepted some degree of variation. He eschewed the traditional regulative principle-based

---

43 John L. Dagg, *A Treatise on Church Order* (Southern Baptist Publication Society, 1858, republished Founders Online CD 1998), chap. 7, sec. 2; conclusion.

arguments of Calvin and the Westminster divines against the use of prescribed prayers and instead appealed to practical reasons why such prayers should not be used in worship, stating that forms of prayer "are objectionable, because they restrain the emotions of the heart, discourage dependence on the Holy Spirit, tend to produce formality, and are not adapted to all circumstances and occasions." He stated of the practice of singing uninspired hymns that "experience has proved their great utility." He stated of the use of musical instruments in worship that it is "nowhere commanded in the New Testament; and it is less adapted to the more spiritual service of the present dispensation." Yet his carefully couched language stopped short of condemning the practice, suggesting in light of his hard-hitting comments quoted above on the Christian's duty to render punctilious obedience to all the commands of God in areas of worship, that he viewed it as a personally disfavored but acceptable adjunct to hymn singing.[44]

Lessons to Be Learned from Historical Application of the Regulative Principle

What conclusions can we learn from history as we seek to apply the regulative principle to worship in our contemporary churches?

One obvious conclusion is that Baptists, of all people, should be diligent defenders of the regulative principle. The regulative principle provides the only theological basis for our Baptist distinctives of believer's baptism and baptism by immersion—the very distinctives that make us Baptists in the first place. If the normative principle were to apply to

---

44 Dagg, chap. 7, sec. 2.

areas of faith and practice, there simply would be no basis for those distinctives.

For example, there is no express prohibition of infant baptism in Scripture. Yet, our position is that only believers should be baptized, not unbelievers and not infants whose parents are church members. The only theological basis for that justification is that we must do what is commanded and cannot do what is not commanded, even if it is also not prohibited. This is nothing more than a restatement of the regulative principle. R. M. Dudley's statement at the turn of the twentieth century in *Baptist Why and Why Not* is worth quoting in full:

> Take the Baptist peculiarity upon infant baptism. They refuse to practice it or to recognize it, because the Scriptures afford no warrant whatever for it. Luther's struggle here was great. He saw that the Bible says nothing in favor of infant baptism. The question with him was: Shall we give it up as our principle requires? In fact, infant baptism had gained so great a hold upon the public heart that Luther feared the consequences of his radical and penetrating principle and hence modified his position and said, "The Word of God does not forbid it and so I will retain it." Zwingli was hesitating and perplexed and failed at last because he did not have the courage of his convictions. The Baptists said, "We will stand by the principle. The Word of God does not authorize the baptism of infants but only of believers.[45]

Similarly, there is no express biblical prohibition of the sprinkling or pouring modes of baptism. Yet, we Baptists

45 Dudley, "The Distinctive Baptist Way," 28–29.

justify our belief that the proper mode of baptism is by immersion by rightly pointing out that, in Bible times, baptism by its very nature involved immersion. The very word *baptizo* means "to immerse." But again, underlying our argument is the unstated assumption that we must do what is commanded and cannot do what is not commanded, even if it is also not prohibited. As C. A. Stakely put it in *Baptist Why and Why Not*, "With us, baptism is not in a mode, but in an act—a specific, definite act, a well-designed, God-appointed act, a truth-proclaiming act—from which one cannot diverge and maintain the rite itself."[46] R. M. Dudley put it this way:

> I am frank to say for myself, that if it were a matter left to our choice whether we should immerse or sprinkle, while immersion is a beautiful and significant ordinance and sprinkling is a meaningless ceremony, still I would give up immersion rather than divide Christendom on a mere rite. I say if it were left to our choice. But it has never been left to our choice. And when others say that they will change the ordinance, the question between them and us is, not what is the true baptism but whether there is any right or authority to change it.[47]

In other words, the very theological justification for what makes us Baptists is nothing more and nothing less than the regulative principle. To quote Dudley again,

> The fundamental principle of the Baptists is their belief in the supreme authority and absolute sufficiency of the Holy Scriptures; and their separate existence is the practical and logical result of

46 C. A. Stakely, "Why Immersion and Not Sprinkling or Pouring," in *Baptist Why and Why Not*, 42.

47 Dudley, "The Distinctive Baptist Way," 28.

> their attempt to apply this principle in all matters of religion. . . . God's Word is the supreme and infallible rule for our guidance. We must not go contrary to it in any article of belief or in any duty enjoined. It is no partial revelation. By it the man of God is thoroughly furnished unto all good works. This is the fundamental position of the Baptists, and every peculiarity which characterizes them is the practical outcome of this principle."[48]

Therefore, to accept the regulative principle—the "fundamental position of the Baptists"—with respect to a church ordinance such as baptism and reject it for other elements of corporate worship is to undermine the very basis of our separateness and drive a wedge between faith and practice when there really is none.

We suggest the following mode of analysis should be used with respect to any practice sought to be introduced into corporate worship:

Step 1. Seek to understand the suggested worship practice in all its aspects.

Step 2. Ask whether the practice is an event of worship or simply a circumstance surrounding worship. If an event of worship, the regulative principle applies. If a mere circumstance surrounding worship, normal principles of Christian liberty apply.

Step 3. If the practice is an event of worship, ask whether the practice is biblically authorized. This inquiry involves determining whether the practice is

a. expressly commanded,

48 Dudley, 26–27.

   b. authorized by example, or
   c. authorized by reasonable inference in either
      i. the Old Testament precepts not specifically abolished in the New Testament or
      ii. the New Testament.

If the event of worship is not biblically authorized in one of these ways, even if it is not specifically prohibited, then it must be abandoned. Practices antithetical to the express commands and implicit teachings of Scripture, of course, are also prohibited.

The second historical lesson to be learned from our brief survey is that the regulative principle should be applied to worship practices in a common-sense and balanced way. This involves several sub-points.

First, although the Scriptures do teach a perfect system of doctrine as well as all principles necessary for the practical regulation of the lives of individual believers and communities of believers, they do not set out all the practical matters of worship in detail. They instead lay down general principles, along with a rich panoply of examples, leaving men to apply those principles in the exercise of the natural judgment, in the light of biblical illustration, and in adaptation to changing circumstances as guided by the sanctifying influence of the Holy Spirit.

The exercise of Christian prudence, of course, does not mean mere expediency, with a view to rendering the worship of God more attractive to those outside the body or to carnal professors within the church. It does allow, however, a wide range of variation in the conduct of Christian worship.

Second, in seeking to apply the regulative principle, we must not overlook ecclesiastical traditions, ethnic backgrounds, and differing human traits and aesthetic tastes. We must not say that Scottish, French, German, American, Latin, and Chinese believers must all agree on every detail of worship, especially in the types of music they use. Must we insist that the music of the Middle Ages or of the sixteenth or seventeenth centuries is alone suitable for the worship of God? If the old is automatically so much better, why not go all the way back to the first and second century or earlier?

The following story about John Gill makes our point in a humorous way. A biographer records that one elderly church member visited her pastor to complain that new hymns were too frequently being sung in church services. Gill asked her if she knew much about singing, to which she replied that she neither understood singing nor could she sing. Gill then asked her what kind of tunes she would like the church to sing. She replied, "Why, sir, I should very much like David's tunes." Gill responded bemusedly, "Well, if you will get David's tunes for us, we will try to sing them."[49]

Even today, music in a predominantly white church and music in a predominantly black church can be quite different, yet are not both worshiping God? Is there such a thing as Calvinistic music? We must do a better job of respecting each other's differences in the details of worship.

Third, the regulative principle must be applied in a balanced and common-sense way. This should go a long way toward dispelling the objection of some that the regulative principle is too sweeping in its scope and the objection of others that applying it in any form will stifle worship.

---

49 Ella, *John Gill and the Cause of God and Truth*, 89–90.

This is where the qualifications to the regulative principle discussed in chapter 2 come into play. Remember the distinction between acts, events, or things of worship, on the one hand, and circumstances of worship, on the other, in the Baptist Confession of 1689 and the Westminster Confession of Faith? Cunningham says of this division,

> Even this distinction between things and circumstances cannot always be applied very certainly; that is, cases have occurred in which there might be room for a difference of opinion, whether a proposed regulation or arrangement was a distinct thing in the way of innovation, or merely a circumstance attaching to an authorized thing and requiring to be regulated. Difficulties and differences of opinion may arise about details, even when sound judgment and good sense are brought to bear upon the interpretation and application of the principle; but this affords no ground for denying or doubting the truth or soundness of the principle itself.[50]

He rightly warns of two extremes to be guarded against: (1) to stick rigidly and doggedly to the general principle, refusing to admit that any limitations or qualifications ought to be permitted in applying it; and (2) to reject the principle altogether merely because it cannot be carried out without some exceptions and modifications and because some details of application cannot always be easily solved. The balanced approach is to make a "reasonable and judicious" application of it.[51]

---

50 Cunningham, *The Reformers and the Theology of the Reformation*, 32.

51 Cunningham, 33.

Waldron has similarly stated about the same division in the 1689 Baptist Confession: "There are certain minor circumstantial details that God has left to be determined by the light of nature, Christian prudence and general rules of Scripture. . . . Churches may differ as to where the line is drawn between circumstances and substance and parts. As long as each church holds seriously to the regulative principle, reasonable differences should not be made the source of division. We must be charitable in such things, while clearly insisting on the regulative principle."[52]

With these concepts in mind, we now turn to applying the regulative principle to the invitation system.

---

52 Waldron, *Exposition of the 1689 Confession*, 271.

THE REGULATIVE PRINCIPLE

PART B: APPLICATION

Chapter 5

The Regulative Principle Applied to the Invitation System

It is a sweltering summer night in south Alabama. The ceiling fans in the church building rotate slowly, supplying only a modicum of relief from the oppressive July heat. The hum of their motors provides deep background noise to the imploring of the evangelist.

"On the one side, you have God, pleading with you to come to him. Walk down this aisle, come forward, and ask Jesus into your heart!"

The evangelist wipes his brow with an already damp handkerchief.

"On the other side, you have the devil, and he's saying to you, 'Put it off. Not today. The church is too crowded. Everyone will look at you. You're too embarrassed.' A thousand excuses. 'You can come forward another time.'"

The evangelist drops to his knees and looks across the hundred or so people sitting in the pews of the First Baptist Church.

"You must decide. You must choose between the two—God or the devil. Today is the day of salvation. Come take your pastor by the hand, and tell him you want to get saved. Your soul is at stake. The decision is up to you. Stand with me, please."

As the congregation rises, the organist begins softly playing the familiar strains of "Just as I Am." The congregation sings.

> Just as I am, without one plea
> But that Thy blood was shed for me.
> And that thou bidd'st me, Come to Thee,
> O Lamb of God, I come!
> I come!

The congregation sings one verse, then another. After the second verse, the evangelist interrupts the singing. "I want every head bowed and every eye closed. I feel it in my spirit that there is someone here who needs to get saved. If you know in your heart that you are not a Christian and you want me to pray for you, lift your hand."

The evangelist pauses to note the scattered hands throughout the room. "Yes, sir, I see that hand. In the back? Thank you. Yes, ma'am, I see your hand. You can put it down now."

He then prays for those who lifted their hands—that God would help them make the "right decision to come forward" and "give their hearts to Jesus."

After the fourth verse, the evangelist holds up his hand to stop the organist. "Only two people who raised their hands have come forward. You know you need to get saved. Eternity is on the line tonight. I want you to know, the Lord is telling me that, for someone in this room, this may be your last chance to make a decision for Christ. It may be that you get in your car after the end of the service and have an accident on the way home and end up standing before the Lord tonight. Lost! Lost! Sir, come now. Dear lady, come now. Young person, if you don't come forward now, you may not get another chance. We're not going to sing much longer. Come now!"

The "invitation" or "altar call" described in this scenario, with some variation, of course, occurs week in and week out in churches throughout our Southern Baptist denomination. It may not always be as dramatic as this. In fact, Sunday after Sunday, it can seem rather perfunctory, like it is tacked on as an afterthought to a sermon about marriage or tithing or child-rearing. Either way, it is expected to occur as a matter of course. It is part of our Southern Baptist culture. From Billy Graham Crusades throughout the world to small country churches in the Deep South, the altar call has, for many Baptists, become part of the rhythm of their souls. If there is no altar call given, no plea for unbelievers to "come forward," they are unsettled. The invariable questions come:

"Is this a liberal church?"

"Doesn't the pastor believe in getting people saved?"

"Is this even a Baptist church?"

The invitation has become so entrenched in Southern Baptist life that it rightly has been called a Baptist sacrament.

Holding to a tradition unthinkingly without reflection is a danger for many people who grow up in one denomination. "We've always done it that way" is a weary refrain to many Baptist ministers. But to slavishly follow tradition, to follow customary methods without thought or question, is contrary to the biblical admonition to be "Bereans" and search the Scriptures to validate traditional doctrines and practices.

The question that must be asked of the invitation system, as with any other worship practice, is whether it is authorized or permitted by the regulative principle. Until recently, not many people have dared ask this question with respect to the altar call, at least in Southern Baptist circles, out of fear of being labeled soft on evangelism. This is unfortunate. No one should ever have to be defensive for asking whether a worship practice is biblical. After all, at the end of the twentieth century, the Southern Baptist Convention emerged from a controversy over biblical inerrancy with the side standing on the trustworthiness of the Bible victorious. For every conservative Christian, the Bible must be the standard by which any practice is judged. Fear of being misunderstood cannot trump biblical clarity. Thus, here we stand.

In this chapter, we examine whether the invitation system violates the regulative principle. We could seek to apply the regulative principle to a wide array of worship practices, but we chose the invitation system because of its prominence in Baptist life and because there is a dearth of material examining it from a theological perspective.

To use the division of the Baptist Confession of 1689, we must ask, Is the invitation system commanded or otherwise authorized in Scripture as an appropriate worship practice? Or is it an "innovation" to be condemned and prohibited? To answer these questions, we follow the three-step mode of analysis offered in the last chapter.

Step 1. Understanding the Worship Practice: What Is the Invitation System?

To analyze the validity of the invitation system, we want to firmly understand precisely what the invitation system is and what it is not.

What is the invitation system? To answer this question, we turn to two of the more well-written books defending what their authors simply call the "invitation." In *The Effective Invitation*, Alan Streett calls the invitation an appeal to unconverted individuals "to demonstrate their sincerity by taking a public stand for Christ before friends, relatives, neighbors, and even enemies."[1] In *Giving a Good Invitation*, Roy Fish calls it "an appeal to someone to accept the benefits of the Christian gospel." This includes "prescribing some specific action in the way of external expression of positive response."[2]

The invitation system, then, consists of an altar call, the practice of requiring those who want to respond to the gospel to perform some physical act to come to Christ in faith and repentance. It involves requiring inquirers to walk down an aisle in a church, to "come forward" to the front to receive Christ. The invitation system, however, involves not only extending the altar call but also praying the "sinner's prayer" with those who come forward and giving immediate verbal assurance that one is now saved based on the sincerity of the prayer.

Proponents of the invitation system tend to want to merge the specific requirement of the invitation system that the inquirer take some overt action with the general idea of an invitation—that an inquirer comes to Christ in faith and repentance. Thus, Fish says that the invitation is "more encompassing" than the appeal to an overt act in response to the gospel proclamation. He says it "includes any kind of appeal to repent and affirmatively respond to Jesus Christ."[3]

---

1 R. Alan Streett, *The Effective Invitation: A Practical Guide for the Pastor* (Old Tappan, N.J.: Fleming H. Revell, 1984), 55.

2 Roy J. Fish, *Giving a Good Invitation* (Nashville: Broadman, 1974), 7.

3 Fish, 7.

But in discussing the invitation system, it is important to be rigorous in our analysis and to separate the various components of the system so they may be clearly examined.

The invitation system is, first of all, to be distinguished from the gospel message. The gospel is the message we declare. To quote *The Gospel of Jesus Christ: An Evangelical Celebration*, it is "news, good news: the best and most important news that any human being ever hears." It "declares the only way to know God in peace, love and joy." That way is "through the reconciling death of Jesus Christ the risen Lord."

The gospel declares that this Jesus is "the Son of God and God the Son, the second person of the Holy Trinity, whose incarnation, ministry, death, resurrection, and ascension fulfilled the Father's saving will." The gospel declares that Jesus Christ is "the living Savior, Master, Life, and Hope of all who put their trust in him." It tells that "the eternal destiny of all people depends on whether they are savingly related to Jesus Christ."[4]

The gospel declares that Jesus, the pre-existent, eternal second person of the Trinity, put on human flesh and became a man, the God-man. He lived a perfect life, obeying God's laws perfectly, the only man to ever do so. This Jesus was sent by the Father to be "the Savior of the world," and it is through him alone "that God's one and only plan of salvation

---

4 The quotations regarding the gospel in this and the following four paragraphs are from "The Gospel of Jesus Christ: An Evangelical Celebration," reproduced in R.C. Sproul, *Getting the Gospel Right* (Grand Rapids: Baker Books, 1999), 99–107. "The Gospel of Jesus Christ" is a carefully crafted statement regarding the gospel and justification drafted by John Ankerberg, John Armstrong, Timothy George, J. I. Packer, Erwin Lutzer, R. C. Sproul, D. A. Carson, and David Wells, among others, and has been endorsed by a broad cross-section of evangelical leaders.

is implemented." Jesus "paid our penalty in our place on his cross, satisfying the retributive demands of divine justice by shedding his blood in sacrifice and so making possible justification for all who trust in him." He thus achieved ransom, reconciliation, redemption, and propitiation for his people. His death secures for his people a restored relationship with God that brings pardon and peace, acceptance and access, and adoption into God's family.

The gospel declares that God's justification of those who believe is "a decisive transition, here and now, from a state of condemnation and wrath because of their sins to one of acceptance and favor by virtue of Jesus' flawless obedience culminating in his voluntary sin-bearing death." As believers' sins were imputed to Christ on the cross, Christ's righteousness is imputed to us. All we bring to the transaction is our guilt and our need for righteousness.

The gospel declares that faith itself is a gift of God, the "fruit of God's grace." It declares that "the moment we truly believe in Christ, the Father declares us righteous in him and begins conforming us to his likeness." We are justified through faith alone, but faith is not alone. It shows itself in "growing obedience to the divine commands."

The gospel declares that salvation is "from the guilt of sin in the past, the power of sin in the present, and the presence of sin in the future." What we enjoy now is simply a foretaste of the fullness to come. While on this earth, believers are called on to "serve their Lord and each other in love, to share in the fellowship of Jesus' sufferings, and to work together to make Christ known to the whole world."

Finally, the gospel is a summons to faith and repentance. God commands men everywhere to repent (Acts 17:30). His commandment is that we should believe on the name of his Son, Jesus Christ (1 John 3:23). Both faith and repentance are acts of the whole man. Faith is more than mental assent; it is the casting and resting of oneself and one's confidence on Christ and his promises of mercy. Repentance is more than a change of mind; it is a change of heart and life. As J. I. Packer so cogently put it in his classic work *Evangelism and the Sovereignty of God*, the demand is for faith as well as repentance and for repentance as well as faith: "Mere credence without trusting, and mere remorse without turning, do not save."[5]

This summary makes clear the distinction between the gospel and the invitation system. The gospel is the message itself that in Christ, there is salvation. It includes a command, true, but the command is not to perform some physical act, such as walking down a church aisle, but to faith and repentance.

This point cannot be overemphasized: the invitation system is to be distinguished from the practice of inviting hearers to respond to the gospel message by faith and repentance. Everyone except hyper-Calvinists believes gospel invitations to faith should and must be given. Every preacher must engage in both proclamation and invitation. Moreover, the invitation we give can be no different from that of our Lord: "Come to me, all who labor and are heavy laden, and I will give you rest. Take my yoke upon you, and learn from me, for I am gentle and lowly in heart, and you will find rest for your souls. For my yoke is easy, and my burden is light." (Matt. 11:28–30).

5 J. I. Packer, *Evangelism and the Sovereignty of God* (Downers Grove, IL: IVP, 1961), 70–71.

We do not want to be misunderstood on this point. We fervently believe people should be invited to come to Christ, not just at the end of a sermon but before, during, and after the sermon. They should be invited to faith and repentance before, during, and after the worship service. They should be invited to come to Christ throughout the week, on the weekend, in the morning, in the evening, at whatever time, wherever they are. Today is the day of salvation! Repent and believe! Those are the proclamations of every true Christian and every faithful preacher. That is beyond any doubt for all who believe and accept the authority of Scripture.

We believe in giving an invitation to respond to the gospel message in faith and repentance because, like all evangelical Calvinists, we adhere to human responsibility to believe. For example, in an 1849 sermon, Basil Manly Sr. rightly declared, "Faith is the key of all the other graces—the commencement and token of all the rest. It is, accordingly, commanded, and put as if for the whole. 'Believe on the Lord Jesus Christ and thou shall be saved.' 'He that believeth not is condemned already; because he hath not believed on the only begotten Son of God.'" Manly likewise said of repentance, "God now commands all men everywhere to repent." He concluded, "Let us not, then, give up either the doctrine of human activity and responsibility, or that of the divine sovereignty and efficiency."[6]

It is the appeal to the lost to perform an overt act in order to be saved with which we quarrel. This is a critical distinction. Fish implicitly recognized it when he observed that John Wesley "always concluded his message with an

---

6 Basil Manly Sr., "Notes of a Sermon Delivered at Pleasant Grove Church, Fayette Co., Alabama, April 8, 1849," *Southern Baptist Sermons on Sovereignty and Responsibility* (Harrisonburg, VA: Gano, 1984), 11, 12–13.

appeal for response, but there is no record of his prescribing any particular external form this response should take." He rightly noted that Wesley "didn't invite people to come forward who wanted to receive Christ" but "he extended an invitation."[7] Streett also implicitly recognized it when he commented that Dr. Martyn Lloyd-Jones was one of the twentieth century's "most vocal opponents" of the invitation system but that Dr. Lloyd-Jones himself "did issue an appeal at the end of his evangelistic messages for listeners to repent and believe."[8]

The invitation system is also to be distinguished from the free offer of the gospel to anyone and everyone. The scope of the invitation is unlimited. We thus enthusiastically affirm that God commands people everywhere to believe the gospel. To quote *The Gospel of Jesus Christ: An Evangelical Celebration* again, "We affirm that the church is commanded by God and is therefore under divine obligation to preach the Gospel to every living person (Luke 24:47; Matthew 28:18–19)."[9]

In short, the invitation system is to be distinguished from the practice of evangelism. The two are not inherently linked, as some more zealous proponents of the invitation system presuppose. We do not believe in the invitation system, but we strongly believe in and practice evangelism. It is our fundamental duty as Christians to obey the Great Commission. Thus, our quarrel is not over whether Christians should evangelize but over the doctrinal foundation for God-centered evangelism.

---

7 Fish, *Giving a Good Invitation,* 7.

8 Streett, *The Effective Invitation*, 131, 138.

9 Sproul, *Getting the Gospel Right*, 105.

Some believers who reject the doctrines of grace have a concern that Calvinism will hinder, stifle, and kill evangelism. This is all too frequently a legitimate concern, but the concern is not with Calvinism but with an anti-missionary spirit that uses Calvinism as an illegitimate excuse to not engage the lost. Shame on all who are comfortable in their own Christian world while people are going to hell around them! Shame on anyone who has grown accustomed to not telling others around them the good news that Jesus saves! This is anti-Calvinistic, anti-Baptist, and anti-Christian. As W. M. Harris proclaimed a century ago, "an anti-missionary Baptist then is an anti-Christian Baptist, and from all such may the church of Christ be delivered."[10]

The invitation system, again, consists of the practice of inviting inquirers to take an overt act to come to the front of a church worship center to come to Christ. Any fair analysis of it, therefore, should confine its discussion to this central point. The invitation system was completely unknown prior to the 1820s and was not used by any of the great evangelists of past times. Jonathan Edwards did not use it. George Whitefield did not use it. John Wesley did not use it. Although some Methodists and Separatist Baptists used it spontaneously on occasion, Charles G. Finney (1792–1875) seems to have been the first to regularly invite people forward to what was called the "anxious seat" or the "mourner's bench."[11] Revivalists Dwight L. Moody and Billy

---

10 Curtis Lee Laws, "Why Missionary and Not 'Omissionary'" in *Baptist Why and Why Not*, 70.

11 Advocates of the invitation system sometimes argue that the altar call was used throughout church history. Such an argument improperly equates the altar call with (1) evangelism, (2) the free offer of the gospel, (3) the gospel message, (4) conversion, or (5) the biblical invitation to faith and repentance.

Sunday refined it. More recently, Billy Graham popularized it through his crusades. Because the invitation system has produced what many would consider to be successful results, its practice has spread to many local churches.

It is unclear why this physical act is thought to be necessary to salvation. As Iain Murray queried in a pamphlet called "The Invitation System," first published in 1967, "Is the walk forward an outward declaration of an inner saving decision already made by the hearer in the seat, just an 'act of witness'? Why then are they told to 'come forward to receive Christ'? How is 'receiving Christ' related to coming forward? Is there any relation? The most popular description of 'the invitation' as an 'act of commitment to Christ' leaves these questions quite unresolved."[12]

Step 2: Is the Worship Practice an Act or Event of Worship?

The question now is whether the invitation system is an element of worship subject to the regulative principle. As you might suspect by now, we believe it surely is. Worship, in many ways, is a dialogue. God speaks to us through the reading, preaching, and teaching of his Word and through the symbolism of the ordinances of baptism and the Lord's Table. We speak to God through praise and by responding to the preached Word. This is entirely appropriate and proper since worship is intended to be a participatory event. The purpose of preaching is to be God's instrument to move the heart and change the will.

See Streett, *The Effective Invitation*, 81–95. For historical detail on the origin of the invitation system, see Thomas J. Nettles, *By His Grace and For His Glory* (Grand Rapids: Baker Books, 1986), 415–21.

12 Iain Murray, *The Invitation System* (Carlisle, PA: Banner of Truth, 1967), 3.

The altar call is designed to facilitate a response to the preaching of the Word—the chief response, the response of saving faith. Fish writes, "The good news is incomplete without an appeal to respond."[13] This response is supposed to occur as the inquirer walks down the aisle at the end of a sermon and then prays the sinner's prayer. Moreover, because it occurs at the conclusion of the preaching, it acts as a conclusion, or at least climax, to the worship service. In these circumstances, there can be no real question that the altar call is intended to invoke a profound—indeed, the paramount—act or event of worship.

Step 3: Is the Worship Practice Authorized by Scripture?

The next step is to determine whether the invitation system is authorized by either express command of Scripture, biblical example, or reasonable inference. We begin this inquiry by examining the major justifications for the post-sermonic altar call offered by its proponents.

Defenders of the invitation system usually put forth two or three scriptural justifications and one psychological justification for its use. We will examine each in turn.

Justification # 1: Christ called people publicly.

Some assert that Christ always called people publicly, and they cite in support such texts as "Follow me" or "Come unto me" (e.g., Matt 4:19; 11:28; Mark 2:14). Others cite Jesus's command to Zacchaeus to come down from the tree in Luke 19. But as Iain Murray has cogently responded,

---

13 Fish, *Giving a Good Invitation*, 10.

> What does "Follow me" or "Come unto me" mean from the lips of the Son of God? Are these primarily directions which require a physical and local movement? That it might sometimes include the local aspect (like Zacchaeus' descent from the tree) is clear enough from the gospel narratives, but even in the days of Christ's visible presence a spiritual identification with Him by repentance and faith was clearly the fundamental sense of the words, and once He was no longer physically present, there could be no other sense. No man can now come to Jesus with his feet, and even when He was upon earth, a coming to Him in that way never accomplished what it is now implied may be accomplished by those who walk to the front. There is no parallel between the modern appeal and the Lord's words.[14]

Tom Nettles makes the same point from a different angle in his seminal work on the doctrines of grace in Baptist life, *By His Grace and for His Glory*. There, he points out that Jesus's invitations in passages such as Matthew 11 and John 6 are actually designed to assure sinners they can indeed be saved because it is God who irresistibly draws those whom he has elected to himself.[15]

In both these passages, for example, Jesus did two things. He first declared that only God's sovereign activity provides anyone with saving faith. Thus, in Matthew 11:27, Jesus said, "All things have been committed to me by my Father. No one knows the Son except the Father, and no one knows the Father except the Son and those to whom the Son chooses to reveal him" (NIV). In John 6:65, Jesus declared, "No one

---

14 Fish, 7.

15 Nettles, *By His Grace and for His Glory*, 422–424.

can come to me unless the Father has enabled them" (NIV). Jesus then assured that all who come to him as a result of the effectual call of the Spirit would be accepted. It is to this person who has come to the end of himself and who desires mercy from Christ that Jesus comforts with his words, "Come to me, all you who are weary and burdened, and I will give you rest. Take my yoke upon you and learn from me, for I am gentle and humble in heart, and you will find rest for your souls" (NIV). It is to this person that Jesus said in John 6:37, "All those the Father gives me will come to me, and whoever comes to me I will never drive away" (NIV).

Nettles points out that the passages in this first category of invitations do not justify the use of altar calls but instead discourage them. "The consistent preaching of the Word of God will draw and keep those who sincerely want to learn of Christ and who realize he has the words of eternal life. The others must be allowed to go away. The one is easily distinguished from the other over the long term, but the public altar call tends to eliminate the opportunity for such discernment."[16]

Justification # 2: It provides the opportunity for a public profession of faith.

Others who defend the invitation system cite verses like Matthew 10:32–33, "So everyone who acknowledges me before men, I also will acknowledge before my Father who is in heaven, but whoever denies me before men, I also will deny before my Father who is in heaven." R. T. Kendall points to Genesis 14:22–23 as the root of what he calls a "public pledge." In a similar vein, Roy Fish cites Moses's declaration to the Israelites when he came down from Mount Sinai and

16 Nettles, 423.

found the people worshiping a golden calf: "Who is on the Lord's side? Come to me" (Ex. 32:26).

The problem with these citations is that a public stand for the Lord or a confession of Christ before men is a mark of a person already converted, not an act by which a person becomes a Christian. As Nettles rightly observes, "Baptism, incorporation into a believing group, regular worship and fellowship with other believers, and day-to-day pursuit of holiness and acts of Christian love—all these have the character of confessing Christ before men and are specifically commanded, as well as notably exemplified in Scripture. Where is either mandate or example of the engineered call to 'come to the front' stated as an act of obedience to God's call to repentance?"[17]

The altar call actually reverses the biblical order. In proper order, first comes salvation, and then comes a profession of faith, beginning in the act of baptism. Under the altar call approach, however, the "profession of faith" in the form of walking down the aisle precedes salvation. This is perverse. As Murray once again rightly remarks, "To confess Christ by coming forward is the spiritual duty of a Christian. It is no part of the gospel to say that compliance with certain outward duties will help us to become Christians. Yet the whole invitation system inevitably gives the impression that 'confessing Christ' by moving forward is in order to conversion."[18]

Justification # 3: Peter gave an altar call in Acts 2:40.

Some proponents of the invitation system assert that Peter gave an altar call at the conclusion of his Pentecost sermon:

---

17 Nettles, 414.

18 Murray, *The Invitation System*, 8.

"With many other words he warned them; and he pleaded with them, 'Save yourselves from this corrupt generation.'" (Acts 2:40 NIV). The Greek word used here for "pleaded" ("exhorted" in the KJV) is *parakaleo*. Both Fish and Streett contend that this word means "to call to oneself" and that this definition "certainly represents a New Testament basis for a public invitation."[19]

Although the word can have that meaning in some contexts, there is no evidence that, in the context of Acts 2:40, Peter's exhortation to faith was accompanied by a request for an overt act. According to the *Theological Dictionary of the New Testament*, *parakaleo* in the context of Acts 2:40 refers to "exhortation by the Word proclaimed in the power of the Holy Ghost." It refers to "the wooing proclamation of salvation in the apostolic preaching." There is, then, "the obligation inherent in the message of salvation," but in this passage, Peter is giving a biblical invitation to faith and repentance, not a request that those who want to repent and believe, but have not yet done so, take some overt act such as coming forward to stand beside the apostle.[20] Bauer, Gingrich, and Danker agree, stating in their lexicon that the meaning of *parakaleo* in Acts 2:40 is "appeal to, urge, exhort, encourage."[21] In sum, Acts 2:40 does not support the practice of an altar call.

---

19 Fish, *Giving a Good Invitation*, 13; see also Streett, *The Effective Invitation*, 63.

20 Otto Schmitz, "Parakaleo and paraklesis in the NT," in Gerhard Kittel and Gerhard Friedrich, *The Theological Dictionary of the New Testament*, (Grand Rapids: Eerdmans, 1964; Logos Library System Electronic Database, 2000).

21 Walter Bauer, F. Wilbur Gingrich, and Frederick W. Danker, *A Greek-English Lexicon of the New Testament and Other Early Christian Literature* (Chicago: University of Chicago Press, 1979; Logos Library System Electronic Database), s.v. "parakeleo."

Justification # 4: It promotes true faith by emphasizing that a decision must be made.

Yet another justification given by defenders of the invitation system is that, psychologically speaking, a step made publicly is more likely to be decisive and irrevocable. Fish says, "There is psychological soundness in coming forward. It is a strengthening factor to men to give them the opportunity to openly declare what they are doing in their hearts."[22]

To our minds, however, the very opposite is true. We believe the invitation system actually tends to create false professors. It assumes that coming to Christ equals walking down a church aisle. It equates man's responsibility to believe with an ability to believe. It presumes that man's decision must precede the regenerating work of the Holy Spirit. This is theologically inaccurate. Scripturally speaking, an ability to believe comes only when the Holy Spirit effectually calls those who will believe. Faith itself is a gift from God (Eph. 2:8; Phil. 1:29). Only those who are called are justified, and all who are called are justified (Rom. 8:29–30).

These justifications, boiled down to their essence, lead to the contention that the whole Bible is an invitation to Christ and this general invitation is not incompatible with an appeal to walk the aisle at the end of a service. But again, this confuses the spiritual invitation, which is pervasive throughout the fabric of Scripture, with a physical act not mentioned anywhere in Scripture.

If the explicit Scriptures commonly offered for the altar call do not support its use, as we believe to be the case, it remains to determine whether the altar call has any implicit

---

22 Fish, *Giving a Good Invitation*, 19.

biblical support, either by example or inference. It is virtually beyond dispute that there are no examples in the Bible supporting a public altar call. Fish virtually concedes the point, quoting Faris Whitesell to the effect that "we do not find an exact example of the modern evangelical invitation in the Scriptures."[23]

While it is true that Jesus demanded a decision from his hearers at the end of the Sermon on the Mount, what he required was a spiritual decision:

> And then will I declare to them, "I never knew you; depart from me, you workers of lawlessness." Everyone then who hears these words of mine and does them will be like a wise man who built his house on the rock. And the rain fell, and the floods came, and the winds blew and beat on that house, but it did not fall, because it had been founded on the rock. And everyone who hears these words of mine and does not do them will be like a foolish man who built his house on the sand. And the rain fell, and the floods came, and the winds blew and beat against that house, and it fell, and great was the fall of it. (Matt. 7:23–27)

As D. A. Carson has said about these verses, the Sermon on the Mount "ends with what has been implicit throughout it—the demand for radical submission to the exclusive lordship of Jesus, who fulfills the Law and the Prophets and warns the disobedient that the alternative to total obedience, true righteousness, and life in the kingdom is rebellion, self-centeredness, and eternal damnation."[24]

---

23 Faris D. Whitesell, *Sixty-Five Ways to Give Evangelistic Invitations* (Grand Rapids: Zondervan, 1945), 12, quoted in Fish, *Giving a Good Invitation*, 12.

24 D. A. Carson, *Matthew 1–12*, Expositor's Bible Commentary (Grand

But certainly, these words cannot support a practice calling for a physical decision that ostensibly leads to salvation. There is no evidence that Jesus ever asked his hearers to walk to the front of the mountain or to a synagogue or even to the temple. As Jim Elliff rhetorically asked concerning the altar call, "Jesus nor Paul, nor any other early Christian leader used it. Did Jesus ask his listeners to come to the front after He preached the Sermon on the Mount? Did Paul say, 'Every head bowed, every eye closed' as Luke quietly sang the invitation hymn on the Areopagus? Did Peter have seekers raise their hands as a sign of their interest in Christ at the end of the Pentecostal sermon?"[25] The answer to each of these questions is, obviously, no.

Is, then, the invitation system supported by reasonable inference from Scripture? On the contrary, we believe the invitation system is not only unsupported by reasonable inference from Scripture but also resoundingly unbiblical. There are several reasons for this conclusion. The first is that the invitation system promotes a works-based salvation. There is no dispute that the altar call invites a physical response to a gospel call—yet it must be undertaken before salvation. This is a violation of the classic Protestant distinctive that salvation is by grace through faith, not works, and that works are a necessary evidence of salvation, not a condition prior to salvation. As dispensationalist Lewis Sperry Chafer recognized over eighty years ago, "again, the false or undue emphasis on methods is disclosed by the imperative demand for some public action in connection with conversion, such as standing or going forward in a meeting. Great confusion

---

Rapids: Zondervan, 1995), 194.

25 Jim Elliff, "Closing With Christ," *Heartland* (Kansas City, MO: Midwestern Baptist Theological Seminary, 1999), retrieved from the internet..

has been wrought by the intrusion of such public acts into the condition for salvation—thereby making salvation seem to be by faith in Christ, plus a supposedly meritorious public act."[26]

The altar call acts as a barrier to those who want to come to Christ. They must do something physical in order to come to Christ—that is, walk down an aisle. The biblical approach, however, is to offer Christ without anything between the soul of the unbeliever and the reality of Christ's offer. "To believe on the Lord Jesus Christ is the very opposite of doing anything: it is resting in the work and saving grace of Another."[27] "To put something in between is a practical sacramentalism."[28]

The second reason the invitation system is unbiblical is that it is based on a theological fallacy—that all who come forward have been made willing to receive Christ by the Holy Spirit. Iain Murray uses the following syllogism:

> Major premise: Only men prepared by the Spirit are willing to receive Christ and be saved.
>
> Minor premise: Men willing to receive Christ come forward.
>
> Conclusion: Those who come forward to receive Christ are assuredly saved.[29]

But as Murray points out, both premises contain logical and biblical flaws. The major premise falsely assumes that any willingness on the part of the unbeliever is willingness

26 Lewis Sperry Chafer, *True Evangelism* (Grand Rapids: Kregel, 1919, repr. 1993), 17.

27 Chafer, 19.

28 Elliff, "Closing With Christ," n.p.

29 Murray, *The Invitation System*, 20.

preparatory to conversion and rebirth. The Bible teaches the opposite. Jesus, in particular, predicted in the parable of the soils that false professors would exist. "As for what was sown on rocky ground, this is the one who hears the word and immediately receives it with joy, yet he has no root in himself, but endures for a while, and when tribulation or persecution arises on account of the word, immediately he falls away" (Matt. 13:20–21). The techniques of the invitation system create a temporary willingness and mental consent in the unregenerate that makes them for a time profess Christ, while the natural enmity of their hearts is unmoved.

Fish implicitly makes this very point, albeit in attempting to promote the invitation system. He observes, "A clear distinction should be made between those who are coming merely as inquirers. . . . [A] majority of those who come in response to an evangelistic invitation have not yet had a valid conversion experience when they make their journey from their seat to the front of the auditorium."[30]

Some churches invoke the power of suggestion and "prime the pump" by having invitation counselors "respond" to the altar call by walking down an aisle to go to the front and meet inquirers there. This especially is fraught with difficulties. The presence of counselors walking down an aisle carries with it the possibility of misleading the unconverted and subtly manipulating people into making a "decision" for Christ when the Holy Spirit has not regenerated their hearts. The same is true with respect to having "every head bowed and every eye closed" and asking those who would like to receive Christ to lift their hands—and then urging those who lifted their hands to come forward. But when the Holy Spirit calls a person to salvation, "there will be little

30 Fish, *Giving a Good Invitation*, 38.

occasion to argue and plead, and methods which are calculated to force a decision will be found to be superfluous."[31]

The error of the minor premise is that many who are willing to receive Christ, at the same time, may be unwilling to walk forward. As Murray states,

> For this large class of persons, the theology of the invitation system really leaves no room. It virtually reasons, "If they are unwilling, they would not come forward; if they are willing, they must be saved"—an argument which hangs its entire strength on equating "coming to Christ" with coming to the front and which supposes that if men have enough will to do the one, they can also do the other. The walk forward and the receiving of Christ are both viewed as within the province of human ability, as though there were no essential difference between the ability by which a man goes to the front at a meeting and the power which turns sinners from darkness to light.[32]

Chafer adds, "Public methods which embarrass any person or class of persons may be not only useless but intrusive. There is little gained by inviting all Christians in a public gathering to stand, thus forcing all others into a conspicuous position, causing them annoyance and creating an occasion for prejudice. It is not strange that intelligent unsaved people sometimes avoid meeting where these methods are employed. By adopting such a program, the evangelist or pastor may be hindering the very work of God which he is attempting to do."[33]

---

31 Chafer, *True Evangelism*, 23.

32 Murray, *The Invitation System*, 24–25.

33 Chafer, *True Evangelism*, 23.

This leads us to the third reason why the invitation system is profoundly unbiblical, a reason on which we have already touched: It gives rise to false professions of faith. We know this in our own Southern Baptist Convention. If our status as the largest Protestant denomination is any indication, Southern Baptists perform more altar calls than any other denomination. And according to the SBC website, we now have 15.8 million members who worship in more than 40,000 churches in the United States. Most of these 15.8 million persons joined their church by walking down an aisle. But do all 15.8 million regularly attend worship services in our Southern Baptist churches? A 1997 study demonstrated that an appalling 67.3 percent of this number do not bother to show up on a given Sunday morning. What does this say about the genuineness of these members' professions of faith?

The danger of obtaining false professions is no less true of a variant on the invitation system that attempts to separate "going forward" with "being saved," the "inquiry room" approach. Under this approach, the pastor or evangelist will ask inquirers to walk down a church aisle to meet a pastor, and the pastor then turns them over to invitation counselors who take them to a back room where they "pray to receive Christ." This separation, however, may be more formal than substantive. A pastor in a Southern Baptist mega-church that uses this approach once told me that he frequently prays the sinner's prayer with inquirers who have "come forward," when he knows they were simply responding to a felt need or psychological desire for assistance rather than trusting in Christ for eternal life. Charles Spurgeon, arguably the greatest Baptist soul-winner of all time, spurned its use for the very reason that it too often created false professors.

The following summary, given by Spurgeon himself, of the August 10, 1879, Metropolitan Tabernacle service, is illuminating on the point:

> On Sunday evening, Aug. 10, the regular hearers at the Tabernacle once more vacated their seats to allow strangers to occupy them. If the building had been twice as large as it is, it would have been none too spacious for the crowds that sought admittance. As it was, we packed in as many as we possibly could, and preached to them with all the power that the Lord gave us. The sermon is published [No. 1,489. "The Plague of the Heart"], and may be still more widely blessed if Christians will circulate it where it is likely to be useful.
>
> This special effort was preceded by earnest supplications at the regular prayer-meetings, by the pleadings of a meeting of chosen soul-winners held in the afternoon, and by the united prayers of the pastor and deacons in their private vestry. It was delightful to observe the discipline voluntarily kept up by the Tabernacle friends; for none of them were present, nor thought of being so. There are generally a few crooked folks who will never fall into rank, or agree to anything which approves itself to others, but we saw no specimens of these irregulars, and we are under the impression that we have no such individuals at the Tabernacle. The idea of giving outsiders an opportunity of hearing their pastor commends itself to the universal conscience of the people, and therefore all carry it out cheerfully. The pastor appreciates this loving unanimity, and takes this

> opportunity of rendering his hearty thanks to one and all. Few ministers have to thank their hearers for stopping away, but we do so most heartily, accepting the action as one of the surest tokens of intense unity of heart in the Lord's work.
>
> The visitors for that evening were a remarkable mixture, comprising the workman in his usual garb, the west-end gentleman in the height of fashion, the sober Friend and the solid man of business, and all other kinds of people. The higher and lower ranks were equally well represented; men were, as usual, much in the majority, the clergy were in force, soldiers blazed in red here and there, and the usual church-going middle-class element filled in the picture. It was a great crush, and the atmosphere was dense and drowsy, but the attention was unbroken and the feeling deep. At the close our spiritual sharp-shooters gathered up each one his share of those wounded by the word. *Results, however, are better seen after an interval than immediately after the service. So it has ever been with our ministry. The converts do not rush excitedly into an inquiry room, but they think over what they have heard, and where the arrows have entered the soul, the convinced ones come forward in due time.*[34]

Notice Spurgeon's careful assessment of how conversion should take place. It does not involve an undue "rush excitedly into an inquiry room," where a person is pronounced saved on the spot. Rather, those under Holy Spirit conviction are

34 "Notes," *The Sword and the Trowel*, vol. 5 (September, 1879) (Ages Digital Library, The Charles Spurgeon Collection), 652–53.

given time to think over what they have heard. Then, when the Holy Spirit regenerates their hearts, they show themselves to have been converted by their changed lives. Only then can and should they present themselves for baptism and church membership. (To take the reference "com[ing] forward" to refer to a physical act of walking down an aisle would be inappropriately anachronistic. It undoubtedly refers instead to the new believer's public profession of faith in baptism.)

Two years earlier, Spurgeon provided another glimpse into his concern about the validity of results obtained by the inquiry room with this snippet in the January 1877 edition of *The Sword and the Trowel*:

> Conversions are thought to be easy things by a certain enthusiastic school, and truly they ought to be, for they are soon over. We have known men converted just long enough to become apostates,—a week sooner and they could not have so dishonored the church, for they had not then been found in the inquiry room. Conversion is something more than this. It is a divine work. "Turn us, O God, and we shall be turned."[35]

By 1884, after several years of observing the use of the inquiry room, his view had not changed:

> As to the Inquiry-room itself, we have little confidence in it as a standing institution, or in its results where much is made of it. We might grieve many if we were to say what we know of the dreadful disappointment experienced by those who look up Inquiry-room converts. An

35 "False Professors," *The Sword and the Trowel*, vol. 5 (January, 1877) (Ages Digital Library, The Charles Spurgeon Collection), 38–39.

> immediate interview seems to be an admirable plan for reaching the heart, and so it may be if used occasionally; but the tendency is to force on an imaginary decision, or produce a hasty faith in the room instead of a quiet faith in Jesus.[36]

To be sure, Spurgeon allowed Dwight Moody and other evangelists to open inquiry rooms after services whenever they preached at the Tabernacle. But he never adopted the practice himself. And even the approach used by Moody did not involve having inquirers walk down to the front of the church before sending them to a back room for spiritual discourse. Ultimately, this "inquiry room" approach, whatever its merits in its own right, makes walking down the aisle practically unnecessary and theologically confusing. Why not just say there are counselors available in the back after the service is over who will help anyone who wants to be saved, who has a spiritual problem, or who desires to join the church? It makes the invitation system entirely superfluous.

The fourth error of the invitation system is that it fails to recognize the mystery of regeneration. It promotes the thinking that a movement of God is formulaic and subject to manipulation by the minister. It thus focuses on the technique or methodology of promoting salvation when Scripture is virtually silent on the point. As Jim Elliff has observed, the Gospels and the book of Acts focus attention on the object of our faith, Jesus Christ, and his life and work, when presenting the gospel, without an explanation of the nature of repentance and faith. The Bible is content to tell us only that repentance and faith are needed:

---

36 "Notices of Books," *The Sword and the Trowel*, vol. 7 (October, 1884) (Ages Digital Library, The Charles Spurgeon Collection), 617.

> When the Word is preached and the Spirit is at work, the sinner is brought to conviction of sin and he cannot love his sin any more. He must repent. And when the Word presents Christ as the only hope and the Spirit is at work in the sinner, he sees no refuge for his soul but Christ. He must believe. Where else could he possibly go?
>
> What about those passages that deal with the nature of repentance and faith in detail? Those passages are there for the presumptuous. The Epistle of First John, James and many other portions help the professing believer understand the nature of faith to test the quality of the faith he says he has. But on the main, evangelism, after laying out the awfulness of man and his sin, and the consequence and offense against God, focuses its gaze on Christ and His work on behalf of sinners. And the people simply believe. There is no emphasis on anything else. They just believe—no laboring on mechanics or methods or perfectly worded prayers, or walks to the front. They believe because it is all they can do.[37]

The fifth error of the invitation system is that it provides immediate and possibly false assurance of salvation to those who may be false professors. In the typical approach, immediate assurance of salvation is given to the person who prays the sinner's prayer.

There are a few biblical examples of immediate assurance being given after a profession of faith. Jesus told the thief on the cross that he would be with him in paradise that day. Philip baptized the Ethiopian eunuch on the spot

37 Elliff, "Closing With Christ," n.p.

after he believed and was saved. But the great biblical text on assurance, 1 John, says that at least one key component of assurance is the evidence of a changed life. Obedience and love and continued faith are the hallmarks of assurance of salvation. Those things are not revealed immediately.

Moreover, the examples of immediate assurance come from Christ and the apostles. Christ, of course, is omniscient and knows the heart in a way we humans never can. The apostles also had special authority and received direct special revelation we do not possess.

It is the job of the Holy Spirit, not his human agents, to provide assurance of life in Christ. Romans 8:16 says, "The Spirit himself bears witness with our spirit that we are children of God." The Philadelphia Confession of Faith summarizes the biblical view of assurance as follows:

> Although temporary believers and other unregenerate men, may vainly deceive themselves with false hopes and carnal presumptions of being in the favor of God, and in a state of salvation, which hope of theirs shall perish; yet such as truly believe in the Lord Jesus, and love Him in sincerity, endeavoring to walk in all good conscience before Him, may in this life be certainly assured that they are in a state of grace. . . .
>
> This certainty is not a bare conjectural and probable persuasion, grounded upon a fallible hope, but an infallible assurance of faith, founded on the blood and righteousness of Christ revealed in the Gospel; and also upon the inward evidence of those graces of the Spirit unto which promises are made, and on the testimony of the Spirit of adoption, witnessing with our spirits that we are the

> children of God; and as a fruit thereof, keeping the hearts both humble and holy.
>
> This infallible assurance doth not so belong to the essence of faith, but that a true believer may wait long, and conflict with many difficulties, before he be partaker of it; yet being enabled by the Spirit, to know the things which are freely given him of God, he may without extraordinary revelation in the right use of means attain thereunto; and therefore it is the duty of every one to give all diligence to make their calling and election sure.
>
> True believers may have the assurance of their salvation divers ways shaken, diminished and intermitted; as by negligence in preserving of it, by falling into some special sin which woundeth the conscience and grieveth the Spirit; by some sudden or vehement temptation, by God's withdrawing the light of his countenance, and suffering even such as fear him to walk in darkness and to have no light, yet are they never destitute of the seed of God and life of faith, that love of Christ and the brethren, that sincerity of heart and conscience of duty out of which, by the operation of the Spirit, this assurance may in due time be revived, and by the which, in the meantime, they are preserved from utter despair.[38]

Thus, as Jim Elliff has commented,

> we are to relate the basis of assurance but leave

---

38 Philadelphia Confession of Faith, Chapter 18.1–18.3, quoted in Timothy and Denise George, eds., *Baptist Confessions, Covenants, and Catechisms* (Nashville: Broadman and Holman, 1996), 76.

> the actual assuring to the Spirit. This is rarely practiced in modern evangelicalism. We prefer rather to take the place of the Spirit in assuring the pray-er and therefore seal many in deception. It is not the efficacy of a prayer that saves: Christ alone saves. The well-quoted passage on assurance, 1 Jn. 5:13 states: "These things I have written to you who believe in the name of the Son of God, that you may know that you have eternal life." "These things … written" are the tests in the rest of the letter which give a basis to determine if we are truly converted.[39]

The frightening conclusion is that, when the lives of those who have walked an aisle and prayed a prayer in a Southern Baptist church are put to the test of 1 John, there is no escaping the conclusion that many on our church rolls are still damned.

Murray summarizes the flaws inherent in the invitation system with the following ten statements:

> 1. The invitation system represents an outward response as connected with "receiving Christ" and thereby institutes a condition of salvation that Christ never appointed.
> 2. The invitation system leads those who respond to believe they are doing something commendable before God, while those who do not are falsely supposed to be disobeying God.
> 3. The invitation system treats two distinct issues, coming to Christ and coming to the front, as though they were one, tending to mislead the unconverted in regard to their duty.

39 Elliff, "Closing With Christ," n.p.

4. The invitation system tends to create false professors because it leaves room for those willing to come forward due to a variety of reasons unrelated to salvation—a depressed person seeking happiness, a disturbed conscience seeking relief, a gullible person influenced by the responses of others, etc.
5. The invitation system, by failing to discriminate out the sincere outward response of those who are still unconverted, leads to further unbelief and hardness of heart when unbelievers who have walked forward find that no real change has taken place in their lives.
6. It is possible that a great number of those who come forward then fall away. This gives rise to another theologically questionable practice—the rededication of one's life to Christ.
7. Those who do come to salvation through the invitation system would lose nothing by the omission of the practice and may even grow deeper roots by the seed of grace coming into bloom more slowly.
8. The invitation system focuses unduly on the outward and the immediately observable. It makes the test of conversion the outward act of conformity and not the reality of a changed life afterward.
9. The invitation system focuses on immediate results and puts subtle pressure on those who do not use it.
10. The invitation system misconceives the role of an evangelist. It makes him a "spiritual obstetrician" whose job is to bring about the new birth of sinners through formulaic methodology when this is, in fact, the job only of the Holy Spirit.[40]

---

40 Murray, *The Invitation System*, 26–30.

As we have endeavored to show throughout this chapter, the invitation system is a profoundly unbiblical act of worship. This conclusion transcends other theological boundaries; it is shared by Reformed (Lloyd-Jones, Murray) and dispensational (Chafer) theologians alike. In sum, the invitation system goes far beyond what Scripture commands in terms of the holiest of all worship experiences—coming to Christ in salvation, surrendering one's life to his lordship in faith and repentance.

The only possible conclusion, therefore, is that the invitation system violates the regulative principle as an act of worship not merely "beside" but even "contrary to" God's Word.[41] It follows that the invitation system is not by a long shot a "minor circumstantial detail that God has left to be determined by the light of nature, Christian prudence and general rules of Scripture."[42]

The invitation system is contrary to the regulative principle. Proponents, apparently unwittingly, recognize that fact. As Fish quotes from Faris Whitesell,

> true enough, we do not find an exact example of the modern evangelistic invitation in the Scriptures, but that fact does not condemn it as unscriptural. Many Christian practices and institutions now in use are not mentioned in the Scriptures, yet we do not consider them unscriptural.
>
> We find no references in the Bible to Sunday schools, young people's societies, women's missionary organizations, church buildings, ushers, hymnbooks, offering envelopes, church bulletins,

41 See Westminster Confession of Faith 20.2; Baptist Confession of 1689 21, 2.

42 See Westminster Confession 1.6; Baptist Confession of 1689 1.6.

> communion cards, church pews and the like, but who would cast them all aside for this reason. *Anything that helps us to carry out the principles and teachings of the Scriptures in a more effective and practical way is Scriptural.*[43]

This, of course, is an unvarnished appeal for the adoption of the normative principle over the regulative principle. But as we have seen by now, that appeal itself is unscriptural and historically, at least, unbaptistic. Moreover, it proves too much. Unlike the invitation system, hymnbooks, ushers, church bulletins, pews, and the like are circumstantial details God has left to be determined by the light of nature, Christian prudence, and general rules of Scripture.

Also unlike the invitation system, Sunday schools and woman's missionary organizations are not components of corporate worship. In contrast to these things, the invitation system is not only unmentioned in Scripture but also profoundly antithetical to fundamental tenets of Scriptural teaching about salvation. Thus, the only conclusion to be drawn is that the invitation system has no place in the church that seeks to be biblical.

These conclusions may be shocking to many Baptists who have lived and breathed the invitation system as part of their lifelong worship experience. Yet surely, the touchstone of any worship practice must be its biblical viability and not the degree of comfort we have with it or the amount of time it has been entrenched in our tradition.

The good news is that many Southern Baptist churches are doing away with the altar call. Many "progressive" churches

---

43 Whitesell, *Sixty-Five Ways to Give Evangelistic Invitations*, 12, quoted in Fish, *Giving a Good Invitation*, 12.

such as Saddleback Community Church are abandoning the practice for the pragmatic reason that today's inquirers don't feel comfortable coming down an aisle before a large congregation. Yet others recognize the severe theological problems with the practice. "In the past, the invitation was designed to 'get 'em down the aisle,'" one pastor remarked for a 1998 article on the subject. "But we have to come to grips with the fact that God does the saving." Another declared, "Tell people up front what you're going to ask them to do." He cautioned, "You can manipulate them to walk down an aisle, and you can convince them that just because they've done what you've asked that they're now a Christian." Still another said, "We don't want to manufacture a moment and force people to make a decision. Then, a month down the road, they're really confused, they finally understand what it means to be a sinner, but they've already walked the aisle." He added, "That doesn't mean we don't have a sense of urgency, but we recognize that is a moment the Holy Spirit, not us, needs to control."[44] To those remarks, we say a hearty amen!

Is the Invitation System Salvageable?

This brings us to a practical problem. It is that getting rid of the invitation system right away, even in a reforming situation, could prove extremely destructive to weaker church members not previously exposed to Reformed teachings. This problem may leave the pastor of a reforming church with a serious perceived dilemma: On the one hand, to leave the invitation system in place knowing that it is unbiblical and violates the regulative principle is to act contrary to

---

44 See Marv Knox, "Will the Altar Call Go the Way of Funeral-Home Fans?" *Baptist Standard* (May 6, 1998).

the Word of God and the conscience of the pastor. On the other hand, to stop using it immediately in any form, with or without explanation, risks the displeasure of confused church members, the possible loss of a job, and the end of all reforms being undertaken in the local church. To stop using the invitation system without first providing a detailed explanation as to why also has the propensity to damage the weaker brother who may have been raised on the altar call and who will not understand why it is no longer used.

Is there a third way? Is this perceived dilemma a false one? The answers to these questions depend on whether the invitation system is salvageable in any respect. Is it possible that the invitation system, if used carefully to omit the inference that the person's "walking down an aisle" or otherwise "doing something" saves, can somehow become, in the words of the Westminster Confession, a "minor circumstantial detail that God has left to be determined by the light of nature, Christian prudence and general rules of Scripture"? These questions all turn on how we view Christian liberty as well as the biblical principle of accommodation. To those topics, we now turn our attention.

CHRISTIAN LIBERTY AND ACCOMMODATION

PART A: DOCTRINE

Chapter 6

Christian Liberty

One of the central notes of the New Testament is the proclamation that in Christ, there is freedom. Isaiah prophesied that the Messiah would proclaim liberty to the captives and freedom to prisoners (Isa. 61:1). In Luke 4, Jesus quoted this prophecy as being completely fulfilled in his person. He is the Messiah who came to proclaim freedom for the prisoners (Luke 4:18).

Every prisoner longs to be free. And every sinner yearns to be unshackled from the fetters of sin that bind them. Even though they may not realize it or may fight against it, deep within their souls, they crave freedom. God made them that way. But true freedom is available only in Christ. Thus, Paul speaks of being delivered from the bondage of corruption into the "freedom of the glory of the children of God" (Rom. 8:21). He says that where the Spirit of the Lord is, there is liberty. By implication, where the Spirit is absent, there is not liberty but only bondage.

A. A. Hodge has commented on our freedom in Christ: "This liberty involves the change of nature effected in regeneration and perfected in sanctification, and the change of relation involved in justification. It is a main element in the grace of adoption, and a privilege of all the children of God."[1] In Galatians, Paul exhorts believers to stand fast in the liberty wherewith Christ has made them free. Simply put, Christians have been called to freedom (Gal. 5:13).

What does this freedom entail? In this chapter, we will discuss the nature of our freedom in Christ. It is important to understand something of the liberty we have in Christ in order to discuss next the practice of accommodation.

What Christian Liberty Is Not

Proceeding by the process of elimination, we will first discuss what Christian liberty is not before discussing what it is.

1. Christian liberty is not a license to lawlessness.

The sinner who is not a Christian is alive to the law. He is "alive to its demands, liable to its penalty, exposed to its curse, uninsured against the eternal loss of his precious soul."[2] The Christian, however, is dead to the law. As Paul said, "For through the law I died to the law, so that I might live to God" (Gal. 2:19). But our liberty in Christ is not lawless. Contrary to popular opinion, *law* and *liberty* are not opposite terms. Rather, they complement one another. Jesus said in John 14:15, "If you love me, you will keep my commandments." He repeated in verse 21, "Whoever has my commandments and keeps them, he it is who loves me. And he who loves me will be loved by my Father, and I will love him and manifest myself to him."

---

1 A. A. Hodge, *The Confession of Faith*, 261.

2 Maurice Roberts, "How Are We Dead to the Law?" *Banner of Truth Magazine* 447 (December, 2000): 2.

How important was this point to our Lord? It was important enough for him to repeat three times in the discourse uttered the night before his death, "If you keep my commandments, you will abide in my love; just as I have kept my Father's commandments and abide in his love" (John 15:10).

The apostle John got the message. He repeated the charge in his first epistle: "Whoever says 'I know him' but does not keep his commandments is a liar, and the truth is not in him, but whoever keeps his word, in him truly the love of God is perfected. By this we may know that we are in him: whoever says he abides in him ought to walk in the same way in which he walked" (1 John 2:4–6). Even though we as believers are dead to the law, the moral law is not banished from our lives. It is the believer's rule of life.

Hodge has judiciously commented on this point:

> It is of the highest importance . . . clearly to understand that Christian liberty is not an absolute liberty to do as we choose, but a regulated liberty to obey God without hindrance from man. It is a freedom from usurped authority, in order that we may be the more perfectly subject to the only legitimate authority. It is hence absurd, as well as wicked, for a man to make his Christian liberty to obey only God a plea to disobey God, as he does whenever he violates any of the principles of natural right or of revealed truth which express at once the unchangeable nature and the all-perfect will of God. There can be no liberty which sets a man independent of that will; and this is always the will of God concerning us, even our sanctification. (1 Thessalonians 4:3)[3]

---

3 Hodge, *The Confession of Faith*, 267–268.

Thus, like human responsibility and divine sovereignty, God's law and God's liberty are friends, not adversaries; and as friends, they do not need to be reconciled. They go hand in hand. Christian liberty, therefore, is not a freedom from obeying God's law. It is a freedom to obey God's law. Christian liberty has nothing to do with license.

2. Christian liberty does not permit us to engage in sinful practices.

Just as Christian liberty is not contrary to law, it also does not allow believers to engage in sin. The consistent refrain of Scripture is that believers must avoid sinful conduct, thoughts, and emotions. Only one example need be given. Paul said in Romans 6:1–2: "What shall we say, then? Are we to continue in sin that grace may abound? By no means! How can we who died to sin still live in it?" Sin does not promote Christian liberty but destroys it. Thus, as chapter 21, section 3 of the Baptist Confession of 1689 states, "they who upon pretense of Christian liberty do practice any sin, or cherish any sinful lust, as they do thereby pervert the main design of the grace of the gospel to their own destruction, so they wholly destroy the end of Christian liberty."

In a related vein, Scripture requires not only that we avoid sin itself but that we also flee temptations to sin. In the model prayer, Jesus instructs us to pray that God will "not lead us into temptation" (Matt. 6:13). James 1:13–16 explains, "Let no one say when he is tempted, 'I am being tempted by God,' for God cannot be tempted with evil, and he himself tempts no one. But each person is tempted when he is lured and enticed by his own desire. Then desire when it has conceived gives birth to sin, and sin when it is fully grown brings forth death. Do not be deceived, my beloved brothers."

Avoiding temptation is also the basic point of Matthew 5:29–30: "If your right eye causes you to sin, tear it out and throw it away. For it is better that you lose one of your members than that your whole body be thrown into hell. And if your right hand causes you to sin, cut it off and throw it away. For it is better that you lose one of your members than that your whole body go into hell." These words are intended to be taken metaphorically and not literally; the point is that sources of temptation are to be cut out of our lives.

3. Christian liberty does not permit us to engage in questionable practices implicitly but not explicitly forbidden in Scripture.

We can take the previous two points one step further. Christian liberty does not permit one to "proof text" Scripture and use it as an excuse to engage in any practice implicitly prohibited by God's Word but not specifically and explicitly forbidden in Scripture. Some sinful practices not specifically mentioned in the Bible are covered by larger principles mentioned in the Bible. Question 99 of the Larger Catechism states, "Under one sin or duty all of the same kind are forbidden or commanded; together with all the causes, means, occasion, and appearances thereof and provocations thereunto."

In other words, the Bible not only names certain practices as sins but also delineates rules and principles by which additional sinful practices may be identified. For example, Exodus 21:29 specifies that to let a vicious ox run loose is sin. The principle underlying this prohibition teaches that to drive a car recklessly so as to endanger the lives of others is also sin. To drive recklessly, then, violates Exodus 21:29.

In addition, there are sinful practices not specifically mentioned in the Bible that are nonetheless prohibited by the "light of nature." For example, smoking cigarettes is not specifically forbidden in the Bible. Neither is taking drugs such as cocaine, heroin, or marijuana. Nevertheless, the light of nature tells us that these substances are harmful to the body and that smoking or taking them is sin.

4. Christian liberty does not permit us to encourage others to engage in questionable practices.

Answer 7 to question 99 of the Larger Catechism states, "What is forbidden or commanded to ourselves we are bound according to our places to endeavor that it may be avoided or performed by others according to the duty of their places." This awkwardly worded statement simply means that we are responsible for our testimony. If it is wrong for me to do cocaine, it is equally wrong for my daughter. If it is wrong for me to see a sexually explicit movie, it is equally wrong for my wife. If it is wrong for me to go play the lottery, it is wrong for my son as well. Of course, the Larger Catechism also states that my testimony varies according to my station. I can command my child. I must exhort my congregation. I will withhold advising my unsaved neighbor, choosing instead to emphasize the fundamentals of the gospel. The point is, I cannot encourage others to do what I, in good conscience, cannot do myself.

What Christian Liberty Is

If Christian liberty does not involve license or the practice or encouragement of sin, then what is it, exactly? We believe that, positively speaking, Christian liberty involves five things.

1. Christian liberty involves deliverance from the wrath of God.

It is the consistent teaching of the Bible that all who are not saved are subject to the wrath of God. John 3:36 says, "Whoever believes in the Son has eternal life; whoever does not obey the Son shall not see life, but the wrath of God remains on him." Romans 1:18 says, "For the wrath of God is revealed from heaven against all ungodliness and unrighteousness of men, who by their unrighteousness suppress the truth." Ephesians 2:3 says that unbelievers are "by nature children of wrath."

Apart from Christ, our condition was hopeless. "But God, being rich in mercy, because of the great love with which he loved us, even when we were dead in our trespasses, made us alive together with Christ—by grace you have been saved—and raised us up with him and seated us with him in the heavenly places in Christ Jesus" (Eph. 2:4–6). Oh, we thank God for the "buts" in the Bible! Jesus has rescued us from the wrath to come (1 Thess. 1:10). "Since, therefore, we have now been justified by his blood, much more shall we be saved by him from the wrath of God" (Rom. 5:9).

2. Christian liberty involves deliverance from the power of Satan and the sting of death.

Christian liberty not only involves deliverance from God's wrath but also from the power of Satan. At the cross, Jesus laid down his life so that, through his death, he "might destroy the one who has the power of death, that is, the devil" (Heb. 2:14). Indeed, all those who are apart from Christ are slaves to the power of Satan. But through his death, our Lord "deliver[ed] all those who through fear of death were subject to lifelong slavery" (v. 15). As Colossians 1:13–14 proclaims, "he has delivered us from the domain of darkness and transferred us to the kingdom of his beloved Son, in whom we have redemption, the forgiveness of sins."

Thus, Paul told King Agrippa in Acts 26:18 that Christ appointed him to ministry "to open their eyes, so that they may turn from darkness to light and from the power of Satan to God, that they may receive forgiveness of sins and a place among those who are sanctified by faith in me."

Because of these things, death no longer has its sting. By the death of Christ, believers are delivered from the fear of death.

Also because of these things, the power of temptation is broken. To quote A. A. Hodge again, "The act of justification has consecrated the believer to God. The work of sanctification breaks the power of temptation, God in every case either graciously enabling us to resist and come off conquerors, or providentially opening a way of escape for us. 1 Cor. 10:13. Thus Satan, too, is subject to his power; he helps us to resist Satan and put him to flight, and the excess of his malignant power he prevents and restrains."[4]

3. Christian liberty involves deliverance from the bondage of sin and unto the service of God.

Believers are delivered from the bondage of sin as an inherent principle of their nature. This deliverance begins in regeneration and continues as the believer is sanctified and ultimately glorified. In John 8, Jesus told those who had believed in him that those who continued in his Word would know

4 Hodge, *The Confession of Faith*, 262.

the truth, and the truth would make them free (vv. 31–32). Jesus's listeners responded that they were Abraham's children and had never been enslaved to anyone. But Jesus told them that everyone who commits sin is the slave of sin. In other words, everyone who has ever lived and who does not know Jesus as Lord and Savior is the slave of sin. How true this is! Spurgeon rightly said, "He who serves his own passions is the slave of the worst of despots. Talk to me not of dark dungeons beneath the sea level; speak not to me of pits in which men have been immured and forgotten; tell me not of heavy chains nor even of racks and the consuming fire; the slave of sin and Satan, sooner or later, knows greater horrors than these; his doom more terrible because eternal and his slavery more hopeless because it is one into which he willingly commits himself." But, as Jesus told his listeners, if the Son makes you free, you are free indeed (John 8:36)! "Free as the mere political liberator cannot make you; free as he cannot make you who merely delivers you from superstition; free as reformation cannot make you; free as God alone can make you by his free Spirit."[5]

Yet, one of the great and mysterious antinomies of Scripture is that, in our newfound freedom in Christ, we are still slaves. As Martin Luther put it in his famous treatise on Christian liberty, *The Freedom of a Christian*, "a Christian is a perfectly free lord of all, subject to none. A Christian is a perfectly dutiful servant of all, subject to all."[6] True freedom is the freedom to obey God's will.

---

5 Charles H. Spurgeon, "The Great Liberator," A Sermon Delivered April 17, 1864 (Sermon # 565), *The Metropolitan Tabernacle Pulpit*, vol. 10 (Ages Digital Library, The C.H. Spurgeon Collection), 269.

6 Martin Luther, "The Freedom of a Christian" in *Three Treatises* (Philadelphia: Fortress, 1960), 277.

Thus, we are not slaves to sin, as we were before our salvation. No, we are slaves to Christ:

> We know that our old self was crucified with him in order that the body of sin might be brought to nothing, so that we would no longer be enslaved to sin. For one who has died has been set free from sin. . . .
>
> But, thanks be to God, that you who were once slaves of sin have become obedient from the heart to the standard of teaching to which you were committed, and, having been set free from sin, have become slaves of righteousness. (Rom. 6:6–7; 17–18)

4. Christian liberty involves deliverance from the authority of men.

The Christian belongs to Christ. We have been bought with a price. God alone is the Lord of each person's conscience (James 4:12; Rom. 14:4). Consequently, Christian liberty means that no man can impose any restraints on the believer's conscience beyond those set forth in the Word of God. This aspect of Christian liberty is sometimes alone called Christian liberty. John Murray points out that "it is only a restricted aspect of Christian liberty that is in view," and to restrict the term to this aspect "would do prejudice to the richness of the concept."[7]

The conscience is an internal awareness that a proposed act does or does not conform to an ideal of right and wrong.

7 John Murray, "The Weak and the Strong" in *Collected Writings of John Murray* (Carlisle, PA: Banner of Truth, 1982), 4:142–43.

It is the part of a person that distinguishes between the morally right and wrong, which passes judgment on the person's acts and which executes that judgment within the soul.[8] If a person acts in conformity to what he believes is good, his conscience is void of offense. If he commits evil, his conscience plagues him. However, if he repeatedly commits evil, he can defile and sear his conscience so that its convicting power dissipates over time.

The conscience is part of the image of God in man. But because we are fallen creatures, it is not a safe guide in all things. The old saying "Let your conscience be your guide" is a dangerous one. The conscience may or may not be following the correct standard of right and wrong. If the conscience's standard is not a true biblical one, the conscience will not give an accurate answer to a moral question.

The conscience can be a false compass in two respects. If an act is sinful but the conscience does not accept the biblical standard of sin, the conscience will not feel guilt, as it should in this circumstance. Conversely, if an act is not sinful but the conscience falsely believes it is, it will produce false guilt where it should not exist.

This is why church-made rules, traditions, and the teachings of men, which by definition are over and above biblical precepts, should not be imposed on people. When a person fails to comply with the man-made rule but has been taught that this failure is sinful, the conscience produces false guilt. But there is good news! Christ came to set us free from the bondage of the traditions of man. For God alone is Lord of the conscience, and he alone has the only true standard to

8 See A. M. Rehwinkel, "Conscience" in Walter Elwell, ed., *Evangelical Dictionary of Theology* (Grand Rapids: Baker, 1984), 267–68.

which the conscience must answer. God governs his people by his written Word and Spirit.

The practical result of these principles is that no one can tell a believer what to do with respect to a category of things or actions called "things indifferent," or in the Greek, *adiaphora*. Adiaphora consist of actions that God neither commands nor forbids and the performance or omission of which is, therefore, an indifferent matter. Because adiaphora are not forbidden, the inference is that they are implicitly approved and therefore allowed.

Scripture speaks to our Christian liberty in things adiaphora in several places. In 1 Corinthians 8, Paul addressed a burning issue of the day—that is, whether it was ever appropriate for a Christian to purchase and eat meat offered to idols. Some Corinthian believers were apparently newly converted from paganism. The "gods" and "lords" of their former religion (v. 5) were a genuine reality to them while they were pagans. In other words, even though they now knew that those gods did not exist, their former association with them was still a part of their experience of reality. As Gordon Fee describes it, they "may tell their heads all they want that the god is only an idol and that an idol has no genuine reality," but "their former way of life [was] woven into their consciousness and emotions in such a way that the old associations cannot be thus lightly regarded."[9] For these believers, to go to the pagan temple and eat meat offered to idols would be tantamount to continuing to participate in idolatry. Other believers in Corinth saw no problem with eating this meat.

---

9 Gordon D. Fee, *The First Epistle to the Corinthians*, New International Commentary on the New Testament (Grand Rapids: Eerdmans, 1987), 379.

Paul came down strongly on the side of those who had no problem eating the meat: "Therefore, as to the eating of food offered to idols, we know that 'an idol has no real existence,' and that 'there is no God but one.' For although there may be so-called gods in heaven or on earth—as indeed there are many 'gods' and many 'lords'—yet for us there is one God, the Father, from whom are all things and for whom we exist, and one Lord, Jesus Christ, through whom are all things and through whom we exist" (1 Cor. 8:4–6). Paul's emphasis is marvelously Trinitarian. In saying there is "but one God" and "one Lord," Paul, according to Fee, focuses on "the uniqueness of the only God." He then identifies the "one God" and "one Lord" as "the Father" and "Jesus Christ." God the Father is "the ultimate source and the ultimate destiny of all things." The Lord Jesus is "the divine mediator, through whom God created all things and redeemed us." Fee rightly states that these two sentences "embrace the whole of human existence."[10] Thus, Paul agreed with those who had no problem eating the meat because there was no reality to the "gods" represented by idols.

But Paul did not stop there. He settled the controversy with an appeal to Christian liberty: "However, not all possess this knowledge. But some, through former association with idols, eat food as really offered to an idol, and their conscience, being weak, is defiled. Food will not commend us to God. We are no worse off if we do not eat, and no better off if we do" (vv. 7–8).

In Romans 14:2–4, Paul again addressed the issue of the types of food that may be eaten, albeit in a broader context than in 1 Corinthians 8. Some people in the church at Rome

10 Fee, 374.

apparently believed Christians ought to be vegetarians. They did not believe in eating any meat at all, irrespective of whether it had been offered to idols.

Scripture does not tell us the basis for their reasoning, although they did not believe abstaining was necessary for salvation. Most probably, Thomas Schreiner is right in suggesting they were Jewish Christians who "believed that one would be a stronger or better Christian if one observed their prescriptions."[11] Others in the Roman church believed there was absolutely nothing wrong with a good steak or burger!

Paul responded: "One person believes he may eat anything, while the weak person eats only vegetables" (Rom. 14:2). In other words, the meat-eaters were right. The vegetarians' inability to eat meat indicated a weakness in their faith. They still believed the ritual obligations of the law should be followed. They had not yet allowed their faith to permeate all areas of their lives.

Nevertheless, Paul cautioned the meat-eaters not to judge or look down at the vegetarians:

> As for the one who is weak in faith, welcome him.
> . . .
>
> Let not the one who eats despise the one who abstains, and let not the one who abstains pass judgment on the one who eats, for God has welcomed him. Who are you to pass judgment on the servant of another? It is before his own master that he stands or falls. And he will be upheld, for the Lord is able to make him stand. (vv. 1, 3–4)

---

11 Thomas Schreiner, *Romans,* Baker Exegetical Commentary on the New Testament (Grand Rapids: Baker Book House, 1998), 714.

In verses 5–6, Paul addressed another controversial issue, that of Jewish feast days and fast days. The weak Christians believed these ceremonies had abiding significance. The strong believers recognized that they had been abrogated. Paul again agreed with the strong, declaring that believers were free to observe or ignore them: "One person esteems one day as better than another, while another esteems all days alike. Each one should be fully convinced in his own mind. The one who observes the day, observes it in honor of the Lord. The one who eats, eats in honor of the Lord, since he gives thanks to God, while the one who abstains, abstains in honor of the Lord and gives thanks to God."

Although Paul in each of these cases went on to address whether the stronger believers should exercise their freedom by refraining from eating to protect the weaker brother, we will reserve discussion of that point to the next chapter. The point here is that each of the disputed points, to Paul, was adiaphora. Adherents to both sides of each dispute could be free in their consciences to continue to hold to their position.

In areas of sin or temptation, of course, believers have a duty to obey the commands of God. They also have a duty to instruct others to obey the commands of God. In the area of "things indifferent," however, the church is not permitted to regulate the conduct of individual Christians. Since things indifferent are not sinful in and of themselves, a Christian is free to use them or not use them as a matter of discretion, except when there is some special reason to abstain from their use. As Paul said in Romans 14:5 and 22, "one person esteems one day as better than another, while another esteems all days alike. Each one should be fully convinced in his own mind. . . . Blessed is the one who has not reason to pass judgment on himself for what he approves."

In church history, the Roman Catholic Church held as a matter of doctrine that whatever is not forbidden in Scripture is permissible. But as a matter of practice, Rome had greatly restricted that liberty by numerous ecclesiastical decrees. Thus, in seeking to reform the church, Martin Luther was a champion of liberty with respect to adiaphora.

Calvin was also an ardent advocate of Christian liberty. In his Catechism of 1538, Calvin wrote, "We are stoutly to resist those regulations which under the title of 'spiritual laws' are in force to bind consciences as if necessary for the worship of God. For they not only overturn the freedom which Christ won for us but also obscure true religion and violate God's majesty, who alone wills to reign in our consciences through his Word."[12] He was extremely concerned that legalism in the church with respect to adiaphora was leaving believers who engaged in indifferent practices with guilty consciences. In *The Institutes*, he said,

> We are not bound before God to any observances of external things which are in themselves indifferent; but are now at full liberty either to use or omit them. . . . The knowledge of this liberty is very necessary to us; where it is wanting our consciences will have no rest, there will be no end of superstition. . . . When once the conscience is entangled in the net, it enters a long an inextricable labyrinth from which it is afterwards most difficult to escape.[13]

---

12 Quoted from John Hesselink, *Calvin's First Catechism—A Commentary* (Louisville: Westminster John Knox Press, 1997), 36–37.

13 John Calvin, *Institutes of the Christian Religion*, ed. John T. McNeill, trans., Ford Lewis Battles (Philadelphia: Westminster, 1960), 3.19.7.

Baptists have strongly adhered to these principles of Christian liberty. The Baptist Confession of 1689 devotes an entire chapter to the subject. Chapter 21, section 2 states, "God alone is Lord of the conscience, and hath left it free from the doctrines and commandments of men which are in any way contrary to the Word. . . . So that to believe such doctrines, or obey such commands out of conscience, is to betray true liberty of conscience; and the requiring of an implicit faith, an absolute and blind obedience, is to destroy liberty of conscience and reason also." The Southern Baptist Theological Seminary's Abstract of Principles adopted this same statement, declaring, "God alone is Lord of the conscience; and He hath left it free from the doctrines and commandments of men, which are in anything contrary to His word, or not contained in it."

Yet here is where it gets a bit complicated. The fact that adiaphora or "things indifferent" exist does not mean there is indifference with respect to any specific Christian's moral actions. Everything the Christian is and does has moral significance. Colossians 3:17 says, "And whatever you do, in word or deed, do everything in the name of the Lord Jesus, giving thanks to God the Father through him." First Corinthians 10:31 similarly says, "So, whether you eat or drink, or whatever you do, do all to the glory of God."

In whatever a Christian is doing, he is either glorifying God or sinning. There is no third possibility. As Andrew Fuller wrote,

> That eating and drinking, and every other voluntary exercise, are moral actions is evident, for we are exhorted, whether we eat or drink, or whatsoever we do, to do all to the glory of God. In an irrational

> being, it is true, these would be merely natural actions; but in a moral agent they are not so, and the manner in which they are attended to renders them either good or evil. Every rational creature performs these actions either to the glory of God, or he does not. If he does, they are virtuous.[14]

This means that, in any given situation, there is a right use of adiaphora and a wrong use. The right use of adiaphora pleases and glorifies God. Conversely, the wrong use of adiaphora in a given circumstance is sin against God. We must always ask, Does this practice in this situation glorify God? If it does not, even in a thing adiaphora, it should be abandoned.

5. Christian liberty does not permit the authority of men in matters of faith and worship.

As we have seen, Christian liberty means that no man can impose any restraints on a believer's conscience. This has special application in the area of worship. As we discussed in the first part of this book, under the regulative principle, in the realm of worship, no one but God can bind the conscience of the child of God. The church has no right to construct its own practice other than what is clearly revealed. In this sense, the regulative principle is simply a subset of Christian liberty for by its application, God has left us free from the commandments of men and not commanded in his Word in matters of faith and worship.

The distinction between matters of faith and worship and all other areas of life is this: in areas other than faith and

---

14 Andrew Fuller, *The Complete Works of Andrew Fuller* (Harrisonburg, VA: Sprinkle, 1988), 2:672.

practice, things indifferent are approved, and the church is forbidden to prohibit them. In areas of faith and practice, things indifferent are prohibited, and the church is forbidden to permit them. Both tenets involve an attempt to remain true to *sola Scriptura* and promote Christian liberty.

Chapter 21, section 2 of the Baptist Confession of 1689 explains that, in areas of faith and worship, "to believe such doctrines [i.e., the commandments of men], or to obey such commands, out of conscience, is to betray true liberty of conscience." The confession goes on to state that requiring "an absolute and blind obedience" (presumably, to these commandments of men) is "to destroy liberty of conscience, and reason also."

John Frame put it this way: "In matters of faith and worship, our liberty from human doctrines is even greater" than in other areas of life.[15] John Allen Delivunk expounds on the point in a 1996 article in *Westminster Theological Journal.*[16] He notes that, from the time of the vestments controversy of the latter sixteenth century, Anglican innovations in worship had given many sincere Puritan believers serious conscience problems. The Puritans believed the use of man-made innovations was not worship. Therefore, they had problems of conscience every time they participated in worship. The Westminster Assembly was formed to protect believers with sensitive consciences. Delivunk explains,

> In Chapter 20 of the *Confession*, one learns that the Westminster Assembly distinguished several

---

15 Frame, "Some Questions About the Regulative Principle," 358.

16 John Allen Delivunk, "Biblical Authority and the Proof of the Regulative Principle of Worship in the Westminster Confession" *Westminster Theological Journal* 58:2 (Fall 1996): 242–44.

> parts of Christian liberty. These are freedom from sin and the wrath of God; free access to God; freedom from the ceremonial law; and, in section 2, freedom "from the doctrines and commandments of men, which are in any thing contrary to his Word; or beside it, in matters of faith or worship." It is this last freedom, called "liberty of conscience," that the authors of the *Confession* used to prove the regulative principle. Because God left men's consciences free from the doctrines and commands of men, the church is forbidden to teach or command anything the Bible does not. This prohibition extends to *adiaphora* as well as sins. In worship, the church is forbidden to add rites and ceremonies to those found in the Bible, because the conscience is to be free of human requirements.[17]

Thus, the regulative principle represents the hallmark of Christian liberty. Because it precludes the use of human inventions in worship, in that area, we have the greatest liberty to follow the commands of God and the greatest freedom from and protection against the precepts of man. This safeguarding of Christian liberty is no less significant a reason for adopting the regulative principle today than it was in the seventeenth century.

---

17 Delivunk, 242.

Chapter 7

Accommodation

What is accommodation? It is simply this: the willing restriction of the exercise of legitimate Christian liberties for the purpose of redeeming people and circumstances which are governed by the ignorance and misunderstanding which results from man's fallen nature.[1] In certain cases, God would have his servants condescend to meet man at the level of his ignorance. Accommodation does not involve a determination of what is the right way to worship but, rather, what is the best way to get there.

The biblical doctrine of accommodation is not well understood in contemporary Christianity. Yet, it is an extremely important doctrine for Southern Baptists and others seeking to minister in the twenty-first century. The doctrine of

1 We are indebted to Dr. Thomas Ascol, pastor of Grace Baptist Church, Cape Coral, Florida, for this definition. We are also indebted to Dr. Ascol for providing notes of a sermon entitled "The Biblical Doctrine of Accommodation" preached at the 1987 Founders Conference in Memphis, Tennessee, as well as early drafts of a chapter of an upcoming book on the subject. We have drawn heavily from those materials here.

accommodation seeks to answer the question: Is it ever permissible and morally legitimate for the Christian minister to forego insisting on change in certain areas until he can make an appeal for change on the basis of biblical instruction and teaching which he has provided?

Everyone who has had souls placed under his charge will struggle with this issue at one time or another. If, in a given situation, he takes a hard-line approach, he may later come to believe that he should have been more accommodating and that his course of action was ill-advised. If, on the other hand, his course of action was accommodating, his conscience may give him little rest since he has convinced himself during sleepless nights that his determination to be accommodating was really motivated by a desire to win the approval of men.

Accommodation and Christian Liberty

Accommodation flows out of Christian liberty. It is the willingness to restrict the exercise of Christian liberty freely and voluntarily.

Recall that in Romans 14:2–4, Paul settled a dispute among some church members as to whether Christians must be vegetarians or whether eating meat is permissible. Paul declared that there was nothing intrinsically wrong with eating meat. These believers were secure in their Christian liberty. "The faith that you have, keep between yourself and God. Blessed is the one who has no reason to pass judgment on himself for what he approves" (Rom. 14:22).

Yet, he also warned the stronger believers who recognized their freedom to take into account their brothers who were weaker in conscience and knowledge. It is important to understand that the term "weaker brother" is not meant to be derogatory. It does not refer to a second-class Christian or someone who should be held in less esteem than other Christians. The weaker brother is a person who is weak in knowledge. He lacks understanding with respect to his freedom in Christ in a specific area (here, meat-eating). The weaker brother is also weak in faith, possibly as a result of his deficiency in knowledge. He has true saving faith, not spurious faith. He is spiritually minded and concerned about following God's will. But he is weak in accepting God's declaration in his Word that nothing is unclean in itself (Rom. 14:14). The weaker brother is not only weak in knowledge and faith; he is also weak in conscience. His conscience screams when he engages—or observes others engaging—in lawful conduct. This is because his conscience is not functioning in the light of mature understanding. He has a false conscience as a result of his weak faith and weak knowledge.

What should the stronger brother, aware of his Christian liberty, do with respect to the weaker brother? Paul gave four specific instructions in this passage.

First, he instructed the strong (the meat-eaters) not to "despise" their weaker brothers (Rom. 14:3). The word used for "despise" here means "to treat as nothing."[2] It is the same word used in Luke 23:11 of the Roman soldiers' mocking, contemptuous treatment of Jesus. Apparently, the meat-eaters had been lording their liberty over the vegetarian believers. This was not the attitude of love Christ required.

Second, he urged the meat-eaters to forebear the exercise of their Christian liberty for the sake of their weaker brothers. In Romans 14:15–23, the apostle cautioned,

---

2 A. T. Robertson, *Robertson's Word Pictures in the New Testament* (Biblesoft: PC Study Bible Electronic Database), n.p. (comment on Rom. 14:2).

> For if your brother is grieved by what you eat, you are no longer walking in love. By what you eat, do not destroy the one for whom Christ died. So do not let what you regard as good be spoken of as evil. For the kingdom of God is not a matter of eating and drinking but of righteousness and peace and joy in the Holy Spirit. Whoever thus serves Christ is acceptable to God and approved by men. So then let us pursue what makes for peace and for mutual upbuilding.
>
> Do not, for the sake of food, destroy the work of God. Everything is indeed clean, but it is wrong for anyone to make another stumble by what he eats. It is good not to eat meat or drink wine or do anything that causes your brother to stumble.

Paul exhorts the strong not to "destroy" the weak with the thoughtless exercise of their Christian liberty. This word, *destroy*, is a strong one. In typical Pauline usage, it refers to eternal destruction. But it cannot have that meaning here because Paul makes clear that Christ died on behalf of the weaker brother. Instead, as Murray states, Paul's use of the term suggests that "the sin of the weak in this instance is a serious breach of fidelity which, if not repaired, would lead to perdition." Paul is issuing a stern warning to the strong that he cannot "take refuge behind the security of the believer and the final perseverance of the saints."[3] Charles Hodge states, "Believers (the elect) are constantly spoken of as in danger of perdition. They are saved only if they continue steadfast unto the end. If they apostatize, they perish. . . . Saints are preserved, not in spite of apostasy, but from apostasy."[4]

---

3 John Murray, *Epistle to the Romans*, New International Commentary on the New Testament (Grand Rapids: Eerdmans, 1965), 2:192.

4 Charles Hodge, *Commentary on the Epistle to the Romans* (Ages Digital

Paul urges the strong to instead forebear from the exercise of their Christian liberty. Love is the reason for the forbearance. As Haldane put it, "self-denial in such matters is the result of love, and when any one will not abstain from gratifying his appetite to avoid hurting his brother, it shows that he is deficient in love."[5]

Third, Paul warned the stronger believers not to tempt or entice the weaker believers whose consciences would not allow them to eat meat. "But whoever has doubts is condemned if he eats, because the eating is not from faith. For whatever does not proceed from faith is sin" (Rom. 14:23). In other words, to encourage the weak to eat encourages him to violate his conscience, and violation of the conscience, even when the conscience does not conform perfectly with God's will, is sinful. As we noted in the last chapter, encouraging someone else to sin is a wrongful use of one's Christian liberty.

Fourth, Paul exhorted the stronger believers to instruct the weaker brothers about their Christian liberty so that their consciences would be informed. "I know and am persuaded in the Lord Jesus that nothing is unclean in itself, but *it is unclean for anyone who thinks it unclean*" (Rom. 15:14). The "knowledge" spoken of here is the understanding of the Christian faith. Those who were strong in the faith were to admonish or instruct the weak.[6]

Until the weaker vegetarian Christians received instruction and had their consciences liberated, however, the meat-eating Christians were to forebear from the legitimate exercise of their Christian liberty. "First, their faith must be

---

Library, Master Christian Library), 657.

5 Robert Haldane, *Commentary on Romans* (reproduced, Escondido, CA: Ephesians Four Group Electronic Database, 1999), comment on Rom. 14:15.

6 See Murray, *Epistle to the Romans*, 2:209.

strengthened, their consciences enlightened; and then they can follow the strong in exercising Christian liberty together."[7] Love of neighbor required no less. "We who are strong have an obligation to bear with the failings of the weak, and not to please ourselves. Let each of us please his neighbor for his good, to build him up. For Christ did not please himself, but as it is written, "The reproaches of those who reproached you fell on me" (Rom. 15:1–3).

Of these last two points, Haldane says,

> When they should receive a weak brother, they should not press him to receive their views by harassing discussions on the points on which he is ignorant. Such conduct would either tend to wound his mind, or induce him to acquiesce without enlightened conviction. Disputation seldom begets unanimity. If a statement of the will of Christ from the Scriptures has not the effect of producing conviction, lengthened discussions are more likely to increase prejudice than to resolve doubts. While, therefore, it is greatly important that believers, who have inadequate views of any part of Divine truth, should be taught more fully the way of the Lord, it is also true that the most likely way to effect this is to avoid disputations with them on the points in which they are weak.[8]

The same advice was given with respect to whether Christians were required to observe the Jewish feasts and fast days, which, as part of the ceremonial law, had been abolished in the new dispensation. In their Christian liberty,

---

7 Douglas Moo, *The Epistle to the Romans*, New International Commentary on the New Testament (Grand Rapids: Eerdmans, 1996), 864.

8 Haldane, *Commentary on Romans*, n.p. (comment on Rom. 14:1).

believers were free to ignore these ceremonies and rituals. But if this caused weaker believers to stumble, those whose consciences permitted them to ignore the feast and fast days were instructed to forbear their liberty:

> The one who observes the day, observes it in honor of the Lord. The one who eats, eats in honor of the Lord, since he gives thanks to God, while the one who abstains, abstains in honor of the Lord and gives thanks to God. For none of us lives to himself, and none of us dies to himself. For if we live, we live to the Lord, and if we die, we die to the Lord. So then, whether we live or whether we die, we are the Lord's. For to this end Christ died and lived again, that he might be Lord both of the dead and of the living.
>
> Why do you pass judgment on your brother? Or you, why do you despise your brother? For we will all stand before the judgment seat of God; for it is written,
>
> "As I live, says the Lord, every knee shall bow to me, and every tongue shall confess to God."
>
> So then each of us will give an account of himself to God.
>
> Therefore let us not pass judgment on one another any longer, but rather decide never to put a stumbling block or hindrance in the way of a brother (Rom. 14:6–13).

Similarly, in 1 Corinthians 8, Paul recognized that Corinthian believers had liberty to eat meat that had been offered to idols. The believers whose consciences permitted them to eat this meat recognized that idols were nothing and there was only one God. Yet other believers, whose consciences were bound, did not have this knowledge. They were "accustomed to the idol"—as a force of habit. Apparently, they were newly removed from idol worship and could not shake the association of eating the meat with idol worship. As a result, their consciences were weak (1 Cor. 8:7).

In deference to them, Paul instructed the stronger believers to forebear the use of their Christian liberty:

> But take care that this right of yours does not somehow become a stumbling block to the weak. For if anyone sees you who have knowledge eating in an idol's temple, will he not be encouraged, if his conscience is weak, to eat food offered to idols? And so by your knowledge this weak person is destroyed, the brother for whom Christ died. Thus, sinning against your brothers and wounding their conscience when it is weak, you sin against Christ. Therefore, if food makes my brother stumble, I will never eat meat, lest I make my brother stumble. (1 Cor. 8:9–13)

These passages describe a sharp delineation between the essence of our Christian liberty and the *exercise* of it. Our liberty in Christ is an inward spiritual reality. It is directed Godward. However, the exercise of my liberty affects others. My liberty is exercised in the presence of the world, of fellow believers. In other words, the appreciation of my liberty is inward and Godward; the exercise of my liberty is primarily outward. As Calvin explained it, "Liberty lies in the conscience and looks to God. Its use lies in externals and deals not only with God but also with men."[9] John Brown

---

9 John Calvin, *Calvin's Commentaries, Commentary on the Epistle to the Galatians*

put it this way in his commentary on Galatians: "It is a very important observation of a judicious commentator [Calvin] that 'there is a great difference between Christian liberty, and the use of Christian liberty.' Christian liberty is an internal thing; it belongs to the mind and conscience, and has a direct reference to God. The use of Christian liberty is an external thing; it belongs to conduct, and has reference to man. No consideration should prevail upon us for a moment to give up our liberty; but many a consideration should induce us to forego the practical assertion or display of our liberty."[10]

The following principles must always guide the Christian's exercise of liberty:

The fear of God. As the servant of Christ, all actions must be motivated by fear of God and love to God. "let us cleanse ourselves from every defilement of body and spirit, bringing holiness to completion in the fear of God" (2 Cor. 7:1). We are to be "submitting to one another out of reverence for Christ" (Eph. 5:21).

Love of others. Though no man may dictate to the Christian's conscience, the welfare of fellow saints must always factor into the decisions he makes. To be sure, the believer is not under an obligation to submit to arrogant or legalistic brothers. But he, in a spirit of love and service, must do all he can to prevent the weaker brother from stumbling. As Paul instructed in Galatians 5:13, do not turn your freedom into an opportunity for the flesh, but through love, serve one another. As he told the Corinthian church in two places in his first letter to them, "take care that this right of yours does

---

(Ages Digital Library, *The John Calvin Collection* CD-ROM), n.p. (comment on Gal. 5:13).

10 John Brown, *Exposition of the Epistle to the Galatians* (Evansville, IN: Sovereign Grace Book Club, 1957), 286.

not somehow become a stumbling block to the weak," and "All things are lawful, but not all things are helpful. All things are lawful, but not all things build up" (1 Cor. 8:9; 10:23).

Compassion for the lost. The use of liberty must always be regulated by its effect on sinners and that behavior that is likely to win as many as possible (1 Cor. 9:19–22).

Watchfulness over the soul. Though free in conscience to use all God's creation, carefulness in practice is demanded because of remaining lusts. Where a Christian judges himself weak, he must avoid temptation in order to persevere in the faith (1 Cor. 9:23–27).

This is the essence of accommodation, the forbearance of the use of our Christian liberty out of love for Christ and others. It is practiced in consideration of the practical state of the weaker brother.

Truth and Understanding

The practice of accommodation is based on the fact that truth must first be understood before one can reasonably expect it to be acted on. As Paul recognized in Romans 14 and 1 Corinthians 8, it is unreasonable to expect a person to act willingly and sincerely contrary to his understanding. He may be coerced into doing something contrary to his understanding, but because whatever he is coerced to do is not an act in which his will wholly consents, it cannot be said to have the quality of true devotion to the Lord Jesus because it is not done "in faith."

Thus, when the apostle Paul prayed for the Philippians that they would "approve what is excellent," he preceded that prayer with another: "And it is my prayer that your love may abound more and more, with knowledge and all discernment" (Phil. 1:9–10). In the same way, when he prayed for the saints at Colosse, that they will "walk in a manner worthy of the Lord, fully pleasing to him," his prior petition was that they "may be filled with the knowledge of his will in all spiritual wisdom and understanding" (Col. 1:9–10). Paul knew it was senseless to pray for growth in their Christian walk without also asking for the blessing of growth in their Christian understanding.

The point is that God does not normally work in the soul of a person independently of his understanding. As J. Gresham Machen once wrote, "What the Holy Spirit does in the new birth is not to make a man a Christian regardless of the evidence, but on the contrary, to clear away the mist from his eyes and enable him to attend to the evidence.[11] It is for this reason that in the New Testament, conversion is not infrequently described in terms of a person's response "to the truth." Becoming a Christian is to "believe the truth" (2 Thess. 2:12–13), "obey the truth" (Rom. 2:8), and have "knowledge of the truth" (2 Tim. 2:25). Paul even described his Roman readers as having "obeyed the form of teaching to which you were entrusted" (Rom. 6:17 NIV).

Appropriate Christian behavior, therefore, is organically involved with understanding. Appropriate Christian behavior involves a translation of right knowledge into proper action. True knowledge is always reflected in sanctified behavior. One cannot expect such behavior prior to the instruction of the truth, which must be first apprehended by the understanding to elicit the appropriate response. Accommodation

11 J. Gresham Machen, *The Christian Faith in the Modern World* (Grand Rapids: Eerdmans, 1947), 63.

recognizes that weaker brothers cannot be expected to fully exercise their Christian liberty until they understand the basis for it, and their consciences can accordingly be freed from misunderstandings, biases, and traditions of man.

Accommodation and Compromise

By now, it should be fully recognized that accommodation is wholly distinct from compromise. We are to accommodate people on the basis of their ignorance of truth but never on the basis of their refusal to acknowledge that which they know to be true. This is an important distinction, and it constitutes the difference between accommodation and compromise. Accommodation involves the maintenance of principles. Under its auspices, principles are never sacrificed for the sake of expediency. Compromise, by contrast, involves the concession of principles. Principles are sacrificed for what is seen to be a greater good. Thus, accommodation and compromise are different in kind, not merely in degree. Tom Ascol puts thusly:

> Accommodation and compromise are two altogether different entities. They are not merely different degrees on the same scale, i.e. with accommodation being 1 to 5 and compromise being 6 to 10. They are different in kind and not merely in degree. At times they may look alike, and they may even appear indistinguishable at points, but they in essence are vitally different. Accommodation and compromise may live in the same neighborhood. They may reside on the same street. They may even be next-door neighbors, but they are not of the same family. There is no blood relationship. And

> while it is sometimes hard to distinguish between them, it is vitally important to do so.[12]

Dr. Ascol uses another illustration to demonstrate the difference as well: Accommodation and compromise are related to one another in the same way that a house cat and bobcat are related. They may share many similarities. At points and in certain circumstances, they may act and look alike. But you would never take a bobcat home as a pet for your children. There are real and deadly differences between the two.

While compromise may have a place in the car buying process or in politics, it is not an option for the Christian trying to be faithful to the Word of God.

Accommodation Illustrated through the Practice of Paul

Paul did not just preach accommodation; he practiced it as well. In fact, Paul is our prime example of how to practice accommodation. He frequently accommodated the spiritual immaturity of others.

In 1 Corinthians 9, Paul explained to the Corinthian believers his own practice of accommodation. He started by describing the essence of his own Christian liberty: "Am I not free?" (1 Cor. 9:1); on the issue of whether he could eat or drink certain foods, "Do we not have a right to eat and drink?" (v. 4); on the issue of whether he, as an apostle, had the right to marry, "Do we not have the right to take along a believing wife, as do the other apostles and the brothers of the Lord and Cephas?" (v. 5); on the issue of whether he

---

12 Once again, we are indebted to Dr. Thomas Ascol for this illustration and the one that follows it.

had the right to expect financial support from the churches, "Or is it only Barnabas and I who have no right to refrain from working for a living? Who serves as a soldier at his own expense? Who plants a vineyard without eating any of its fruit? Or who tends a flock without getting some of the milk?" (vv. 6–7). Indeed, on this last point, he pointed out that Scripture commanded the churches to financially compensate their ministers (vv. 8–11, 14). "If others share this rightful claim on you, do not we even more?" (v. 12).

Paul cherished his freedom in Christ. He has rightly been called the "apostle of the heart set free."[13] He called the one set free from the bondage of sin "the Lord's freedman" (1 Cor. 7:22). In Galatians 5:1, Paul declared that "for freedom Christ has set us free."

Yet Paul refused to exercise his cherished freedom out of love for others. "I have made no use of any of these things" (1 Cor. 9:15). Instead, he voluntarily chose to forebear "rather than put an obstacle in the way of the gospel of Christ" (v. 12). Why? He explained the reason in verses 19–23:

> For though I am free from all, I have made myself a servant to all, that I might win more of them. To the Jews I became as a Jew, in order to win Jews. To those under the law I became as one under the law (though not being myself under the law) that I might win those under the law. To those outside the law I became as one outside the law (not being outside the law of God but under the law of Christ) that I might win those outside the law. To the weak I became weak, that I might win the weak. I have become all things to all people,

13 See F. F. Bruce, *Paul, Apostle of the Heart Set Free* (Grand Rapids: Eerdmans, 1977, repr. 1995).

> that by all means I might save some. I do it all for the sake of the gospel, that I may share with them in its blessings.

Wherever he encountered weaker brothers whose consciences were bound by prejudices resulting from ignorance, misunderstanding, or custom, Paul accommodated himself to those brothers. He willfully gave up the lawful exercise of his Christian liberty with respect to things indifferent so that "I may by all means save some." He practiced accommodation to the fullest extent possible "for the sake of the gospel."

We see an example of this in Acts 21:18–26. There, Paul accommodated some Jewish Christians, at the suggestion of James and the elders of the church at Jerusalem, by submitting to ritual purification. James and the other elders advised Paul that some troublemakers had falsely accused him of having no regard for the Mosaic law. They suggested, "There are four men with us who have made a vow. Take these men, join in their purification rites and pay their expenses, so that they can have their heads shaved. Then everybody will know there is no truth in these reports about you, but that you yourself are living in obedience to the law" (Acts 21:23–24 NIV). Paul agreed (v. 26). He thus put into practice the principle he penned in 1 Corinthians 9:20: "To the Jews I became as a Jew, in order to win Jews. To those under the law I became as one under the law (though not being myself under the law) that I might win those under the law." Paul conformed himself to their custom, not because he was under the law but as a matter of accommodation.

Paul consented to accommodate the Jewish Christians because he knew his credibility and reputation were at stake. If he had decided to refuse the request of James and the elders, many who were theologically immature would have been unnecessarily prejudiced against the apostle. Paul would have then been preaching to those who had erroneously concluded that he had denied the faith of the fathers.

Sometimes the line between accommodation and compromise is razor-thin. Sometimes the same conduct in different situations can be either accommodation or compromise. This is illustrated by Paul's conduct with respect to circumcision. Paul knew that circumcision, in and of itself, was not sinful. As a Jew, he was circumcised. Circumcision was only wrong when it was performed out of a desire to gain acceptance with God through it. Therefore, Paul had no qualms about personally circumcising Timothy, his younger associate in ministry. As recorded in Acts 16:3, he did so "because of the Jews who were in those places, for they all knew that his father was a Greek." Paul, not wanting to prejudice the Jews against Timothy's ministry, anticipated their objections and circumcised Timothy.

At the same time, however, Paul understood that circumcision was not required as a prerequisite to salvation. The minute anyone suggested to the contrary, Paul was ready to fight for the free grace of the gospel. The Galatians, for example, were flirting with returning to pre-Christian Judaism under the influence of the heretical Judaizers. They were considering leaving the full liberty of the gospel for the relative bondage of the old dispensation. Paul called this "another gospel" (Gal. 1:7 KJV). The Galatians were on the verge of rejecting Christ and the gospel. Ridderbos observed,

> The issue is not circumcision as such, as though circumcised persons could not be saved, but

> circumcision as the Judaists were demanding it of the Gentiles as a condition for obtaining salvation. The sufficiency of Christ's work is what is being challenged. True, the Galatians have not entirely yielded to the opponents, but they are being prodded in that direction and seem turned that way (cf. 4:10). Hence it is necessary now to set the whole matter in sharpest focus and consistency, and to see through its implications.[14]

There could be no return to the position of the pre-Christian believer; there could only be a lapse into unbelief. He therefore told the Galatians in the strongest possible terms that if they received circumcision thinking it was a condition of salvation, they received nothing: "Look: I, Paul, say to you that if you accept circumcision, Christ will be of no advantage to you" (Gal. 5:2). "Circumcision or Christ: everything or nothing."[15]

This was not Paul's first struggle with Judaizers over the issue of circumcision. In chapter 2 of his letter to the Galatians, Paul reminded his readers of a prior occasion when he had opposed a return to the dictates of pre-Christian Judaism. After Paul and Barnabas had returned to Antioch from their first missionary journey, some Judaizers had come to the church there and tried to require circumcision as an element of salvation. The elders in Jerusalem had called a conference to adjudicate the issue, and Paul and Barnabas had gone to Jerusalem for the conference. Paul took with him Titus, an uncircumcised Greek Christian whose very

14 Herman N. Ridderbos, *The Epistle of Paul to the Churches of Galatia*, New International Commentary on the New Testament (Grand Rapids: Eerdmans, 1953), 187.

15 Ridderbos.

presence was likely to be a challenge to the Judaizers. During the internal debates among the apostles, Paul argued fiercely for free grace. As he retold it to the Galatians:

> But even Titus, who was with me, was not forced to be circumcised, though he was a Greek. Yet because of false brothers secretly brought in—who slipped in to spy out our freedom that we have in Christ Jesus, so that they might bring us into slavery—to them we did not yield in submission even for a moment, so that the truth of the gospel might be preserved for you. (Gal. 2:3–5)

On this occasion, Paul would not accommodate—because to do so would have been to compromise. The very gospel was at stake. Although Paul was ready to go to great lengths to accommodate, his willingness to do so was limited by the law of God.

Some may wonder whether Paul's willingness to accommodate and circumcise Timothy undermined his main message that salvation is through grace by faith. Not at all. As Charles Simeon observed:

> We must distinguish between an occasional conformity to a rite for the sake of removing prejudices, and an insisting on that rite as necessary. If he had told the Jews that the ceremonial law was necessary to be observed in order to their salvation, he would have indeed betrayed the cause of Christ. If he had even inculcated the observation of it as having an efficacy towards their acceptance with God, he would have then also have betrayed the cause of Christ ... But he merely showed, that if, on the one hand, men were not to be saved by their observance of the law, they would not be

> condemned for it, provided they did not rely on it for their justification before God.[16]

Let pastors, missionaries, and other church leaders beware of being more pious than the Bible would have them be! Let Christians beware of thinking that faithfulness to God involves offending others as much as possible and as frequently as possible. A sincere desire to meet people where they are need not be understood as a spirit of compromise. It is all too frequently the case that Christians, in attempting to be faithful to God by their zeal in promoting his truth, grievously offend him by their lack of love to others.

Accommodation and Sanctification

The practice of accommodation should be viewed in conjunction with the biblical doctrine of sanctification. The Bible teaches that sanctification is progressive. "Like the natural faculties both of body and mind … so Christian graces, or spiritual habits, are developed by exercise."[17] In other words, sanctification and Christian growth are a gradual, lifelong process. There are different degrees of growth, and no believer is perfect in this life. We find "that so long as we are in the flesh, our attainments are less than is to be desired. In our daily reading we fall in with many obscure passages that convict us of ignorance. With this curb, God keeps us modest, assigning to each a measure of faith, that every teacher, however excellent, may still be disposed to

---

16 Charles Simeon, *Expository Outlines on the Whole Bible* (Grand Rapids: Zondervan, 1955), 4:540.

17 A. A. Hodge, *Outlines of Theology* (Ephesians 4 Group CD-ROM), n.p. (35.10).

learn."[18] Some Christians are able to receive more and bear more because they are further along in growth than others. Furthermore, some Christians have more mental ability than others. Some have more formal education, and some have had the privilege of regularly sitting under a biblical and consistently expository ministry. To ignore the legitimacy or place of accommodation in light of the process of sanctification is to deny the obvious.

Thus, the apostle Paul, taking cognizance of the Corinthian believers' arrested growth in a specific area, could say, "I fed you with milk, not solid food, for you were not ready for it. And even now you are not yet ready, for you are still of the flesh. For while there is jealousy and strife among you, are you not of the flesh and behaving only in a human way?" (1 Cor. 3:2–3). Because the Corinthians were babes in Christ in many ways, Paul adjusted their spiritual diet accordingly. He did not want to feed them that which they could not chew. So too could Christ say to his disciples in John 16:12, "I have many more things to say to you, but you cannot bear them now." As the disciples had nothing but his teachings on which to rely, "Christ reminds them that he had accommodated it to their capacity."[19]

Some Christian ministers may say in response to all this, "Why should I allow the ignorance of my brother to deprive me of my genuine liberty?" Our answer is that you may cause your weaker brother to stumble if you insist on the exercise of your liberty. "But why should I be held responsible for his stumbling?" the objector may ask. "Why should not his

---

18 John Calvin, *The Institutes of the Christian Religion*, 3.2.4.

19 John Calvin, *Commentary on the Gospel According to John* (Ages Digital Library, The John Calvin Collection), 537.

stumbling be charged to his ignorance and I be left in the enjoyment of my Christian liberty?" "Is there any sound reason why my freedom should be restricted for fear of offending the ignorant, the old-fashioned, and the traditionalist?" In effect, the question here is, Why should I care if the ignorant and weak stumble?

There is a paramount reason why the true Christian should care. The weaker brother is a soul for whom Christ died (1 Cor. 8:11; Rom. 14:15)! By sinning against him, you are sinning against Christ himself (1 Cor. 8:12). Love is the guiding principle of life and ministry. Knowledge gives Christians liberty to practice things indifferent. But love gives liberty to refrain from those practices for the sake of the soul for whom Christ died.

In sum, every Christian must practice accommodation, without compromise, for the love of the brother and for the sake of the gospel. We now turn to apply what we have learned about Christian liberty and accommodation to the altar call.

CHRISTIAN LIBERTY AND ACCOMMODATION

PART B: APPLICATION

Chapter 8

Applying the Practice of Accommodation to the Altar Call

The question to now be asked is whether the altar call is prohibited in each and every circumstance, no matter how it is presented. Can it somehow become a "minor circumstantial detail" God has left to be determined by the light of nature, Christian prudence, and general rules of Scripture? In other words, is there a place for accommodation when it comes to this well-entrenched practice?

The problem, as we have seen, is that many if not most Southern Baptist congregations still have false assumptions regarding evangelism and the altar call. Even in a reforming church, the congregation may be seeing the light with regard to the doctrines of grace but may not have seen all the implications of these doctrinal distinctives in some areas. The congregation may still be laboring under the false notion that inviting people to Christ is incomplete unless an altar call is given for inquirers to come to the front of the church building. They are weaker brothers and sisters in this area of understanding, laboring under a theological prejudice built up over years of Baptist custom and tradition. Their consciences are bound to an expectation that an altar call will be given after every service. What should the conscientious pastor do? Should he boldly declare that as of next Sunday, there will be no more altar calls from this pulpit? We believe the answer in most circumstances should be no.

First, as we have seen in examining the biblical doctrine of accommodation, learning and the intelligent comprehension of truth must precede the application of the truth. In other words, there is no point in seeking to apply a specific truth unless the truth is first expounded and understood. This may take time, for knowledge displaces ignorance slowly. Thus we read of Paul and Barnabas that "for a whole year they met with the church and taught a great many people" (Acts 11:26). Many Christians, for example, who now embrace the doctrines of grace, once did not receive these truths, and their view with regard to evangelism shifted only after they came to a consistent understanding of these truths. Therefore, to expect people to accept a methodology of evangelism thoroughly consistent with the doctrines of grace without their first having a parallel growth and development in their doctrinal understanding is to court defeat from the beginning. Put differently, a pastor's decision to omit any form of altar call when the congregation expects it is to cast a shadow over the pastor's own theological integrity and judgment. It would put his ability as a spiritual leader into question and possibly jeopardize his ministry in that congregation.

Second, seeking to change a practice contrary to the congregation's understanding could also have a dangerous side effect of raising unnecessary prejudices against the one who is teaching. As the apostle Paul had to take care that he did not unnecessarily prejudice the weaker Christians in Corinth, Jerusalem, or other places, so too must the pastor wrestling with a congregation that expects an altar call to be given. He must be careful that he does not cast a shadow of suspicion over his theological integrity and judgment. To do so would be to put his ability as a spiritual leader in question and jeopardize his whole ministry with that congregation.

Third, the altar call can be "defanged." There is nothing intrinsically evil about people walking to the front of a church building at the end of a service. The issue that must be addressed is the *reason* why people are walking to the front. If they walk forward because they believe they must do so to be saved, there is no Christian liberty, and that misconception must be corrected. On the other hand, when a person is converted, there must be a time and way of expressing that person's desire to be baptized and to join the fellowship of the local assembly. There is no valid reason why it cannot be done in response to an invitation from the pastor. Those who believe themselves to be recipients of saving grace can surely be invited to come forward and present themselves as candidates for baptism.

These types of altar calls do not in any fashion violate the regulative principle. To invite the *converted* to come forward does not cut across any principle of biblical theology discussed in this book. In no way does it represent the outward response of going forward as being connected with "receiving Christ." Separated from the religious significance to which it is often attached, walking down an aisle is neither commanded nor forbidden. Thus, it does not establish a way of salvation not appointed by him who alone has the prerogative to make such appointments.

These types of altar calls reflect the practice of accommodation because they take into account human infirmity without being satisfied with human ignorance. By accommodating the prejudices of the congregation, they provide the pastor with a greater opportunity to minister to the people and, over time, to dispel the prejudices that gave rise to the accommodation. They also might avoid hindering some weaker brother for whom Christ died.

On some occasions, they may even be events of worship, such as responding to the invitation of the sermon to dedicate one's life to missionary service. In other cases, they may be circumstances of worship—for example, coming to the front to pray. The location of the prayer is not important. As long as the implication is eliminated that coming forward is required for salvation, the altar call can serve a useful and appropriate purpose.

Of course, those who may decide to accommodate in this fashion should know that the practice of inviting people to the front of a church building has historically been wedded to a false theology. Does this mean that inviting people forward is so invariably tainted it cannot be used in any circumstances without harm? The apostle Paul was faced with this same question with respect to the practice of circumcision. He did not conclude that circumcision was so tainted, even though the Judaizers were touting it as an essential element of salvation—in direct contravention of Paul's cherished doctrine of justification by faith alone. He was willing to face the invariable criticism that followed and went ahead to circumcise Timothy out of love for the weaker brother. He resolved the question in favor of accommodation and even circumcised Timothy on the very heels of the Jerusalem council at which he argued so vociferously against the circumcision of Titus.

Some may ask how long accommodation should be practiced with respect to the altar call. In answering this question, it is important to remember the proper grounds for the exercise of biblical accommodation. We are to accommodate people on the basis of their ignorance of the truth but never on the basis of their refusal to acknowledge that which they know to be true. This makes all the difference between accommodation and compromise. Keeping this consideration in mind will give us a principle to use in determining just how long we must accommodate a congregation in this matter.

Accommodation should be continued as long as the congregation continues to be instructed. Once ignorance is dispelled, accommodation no longer needs to be practiced. Beyond this general principle, no specific answer can be given. We must wait on the Holy Spirit for enlightenment. It goes without saying, in this regard, that while accommodation is ongoing, it is the responsibility of the Christian leader actively to instruct the weak with regard to the unbiblical nature of the traditional invitation system along with those basic doctrines of soteriology it touches on, such as the nature of the gospel call, the duty of all people to believe, what it means to come to Christ in faith and repentance, and the basis of genuine assurance of salvation.

One further thought on the matter should be said. Inviting people forward, as suggested above, in no way promotes the erroneous and dangerous notion that one's consciousness of faith is a sufficient basis for an abiding assurance that one is in a state of grace. As we discussed in chapter 5, one of the greatest dangers of the invitation system resides not only in the false equating of physical movement with coming to Christ but also in the prevailing practice of granting immediate assurance of salvation on the basis of that movement. The Scriptures speak of believing in vain (1 Cor. 15:2). They speak of those who "believe for a while, and in time of testing fall away" (Luke 8:13). For this reason, those who profess to be savingly joined to the Lord are exhorted to make their election and calling sure (2 Peter 1:10). Any enduring sense of assurance of salvation maintained apart from a consistent Christian walk may very well be a dangerous deception. And yet, inviting the converted to the front of the church building for prayer, as a sign of devotion, or as an opportunity to submit to believer's baptism in no way partakes of this error.

Some may see our proposed solution as fraught with difficulties of its own. This may be. This is a problem we all face when making a decision between difficult alternatives. Rarely, if ever, do people have the opportunity of making a difficult decision regarding the application of a biblical principle by neatly putting all the positive factors on one side of the equation and all the negative factors on the other. Difficult decisions of application involve a process of choosing among several alternatives, each of which may have attractive features as well as perceived unattractive ones. In our fallen world, making a choice between two alternatives regarding the application of biblical truth involves choosing one set of problems over another. Criticism from others may be the problem you choose to accept if you decide to practice accommodation. That was Paul's choice.

Biblical accommodation is certainly not a panacea for all the ills of contemporary evangelicalism and the Southern Baptist Convention. But it is divinely appointed by God as a means by which we may show love to others and lessen some of the conflicts that inevitably come when we attempt to reform a church by leading it back to its biblical foundation.

Robert L. Dabney, one of the greatest American theologians of the nineteenth century, once wrote, "All possible human actions must fall in one of these three classes: (1) actions which Scripture positively enjoins; (2) actions which Scripture positively forbids; (3) actions which Scripture leaves indifferent."[1] Does the giving of an altar call as outlined above come under the category of 1, 2, or 3?

Soli Deo Gloria

1 Robert L. Dabney, "Anti-Biblical Theories of Rights" in *Discussions: Evangelical and Theological* (Carlisle, PA: Banner of Truth, 1982), 3:522.

Scripture Index

Old Testament

New Testament

Acts

Romans

1 Corinthians

Other Titles from Founders Press

BY WHAT STANDARD? God's World . . . God's Rules.

Edited by Jared Longshore

I'm grateful for the courage of these men and the clarity of their voices. This is a vitally important volume, sounding all the right notes of passion, warning, instruction, and hope.

—Phil Johnson, Executive Director,
Grace To You

Truth & Grace Memory Books

Edited by Thomas K. Ascol

Memorizing a good, age-appropriate catechism is as valuable for learning the Bible as memorizing multiplication tables is for learning mathematics.

—Dr. Don Whitney, Professor,
The Southern Baptist Theological Seminary

Dear Timothy: Letters on Pastoral Ministry

Edited by Thomas K. Ascol

Get this book. So many experienced pastors have written in this book it is a gold mine of wisdom for young pastors in how to preach and carry out their ministerial life.

—Joel Beeke, President,
Puritan Reformed Theological Seminary

The Mystery of Christ, His Covenant & His Kingdom

By Samuel Renihan

This book serves for an excellent and rich primer on covenant theology and demonstrates how it leads from the Covenant of Redemption to the final claiming and purifying of the people given by the Father to the Son.

—Tom Nettles, Retired Professor of Historical Theology,
The Southern Baptist Theological Seminary

Strong And Courageous: Following Jesus Amid the Rise of America's New Religion

By Tom Ascol and Jared Longshore

We have had quite enough of "Be Nice and Inoffensive." We are overflowing with "Be Tolerant and Sensitive." It is high time that we were admonished to "Be Strong and Courageous.'"

—Jim Scott Orrick, Author,
Pastor of Bullitt Lick Baptist Church

Additional titles

Heirs of the Reformation: A Study in Baptist Origins

By Daniel Scheiderer

Still Confessing: An Exposition of the Baptist Faith & Message 2000

By Daniel Scheiderer

By His Grace and for His Glory

By Tom Nettles

Getting the Garden Right

By Richard C. Barcellos

The Law and the Gospel

By Ernie Reisinger

Traditional Theology & the SBC

By Tom Ascol

Teaching Truth, Training Hearts

By Tom Nettles

Praise Is His Gracious Choice:
Corporate Worship Expressing Biblical Truth
By Dr. Tom Nettles

Just Thinking: about the state
By Darrell Harrison and Virgil Walker

The Transcultural Gospel
By E.D. Burns

Ancient Gospel, Brave New World
By E.D. Burns

Galatians: He Did It All
By Baruch Maoz

Missions by the Book: How Theology and Missions Walk Together
By Chad Vegas and Alex Kocman

CPSIA information can be obtained
at www.ICGtesting.com
Printed in the USA
LVHW050838311221
707311LV00004B/8

9 780970 524867